An Introduction to Expert Systems

Jay Liebowitz

The George Washington University
Washington, D.C.

Mitchell Publishing, Inc.
Innovators in Computer Education
915 River Street • Santa Cruz, California 95060
(800) 435-2665 • In California (408) 425-3851
"A Random House Company"

To my parents, my wife, Janet, and my son, Jason.

Cover Design: Henry Breuer
Desktop Publishing Service: Arizona Publication Service
Printed by: R.R. Donnelley
Product Development: Raleigh S. Wilson
Sponsoring Editor: Raleigh S. Wilson

Printed in the United States of America

  10 9 8 7 6 5 4 3 2 1

Library of Congress Card Catalog No.: 87-91966

ISBN: 0-394-39141-1

Brief Table of Contents

Detailed Table of Contents

Preface

The computing society has moved from the data age through the information age to the knowledge age. Machines not only store, manipulate, and retrieve data and information aiding the decision maker, but increasingly are programmed to make specific decisions. These decision making programs are part of the general area of artificial intelligence. A subset of this field is expert systems—an area where computer programs are developed that emulate human experts in specific tasks. Over the last five years, commercial interest has grown in the area, with expert systems being developed for medical diagnosis to tax planning to computer configuration. Most of this work, however, is still in the research or field prototype stage. Much more work, both in basic and applied research, is needed to make expert systems commercially successful and accessible to a larger audience.

Why this Book Is Needed

This book was written to help readers better understand expert systems, and to provide practical suggestions in developing expert systems. It could equally be used by the business manager, executive, or engineer who wants a reasonable and nontechnical introduction to expert systems. The book is also useful to future knowledge engineers, as it provides practical guidelines to building expert systems. Many of the expert systems books written today, I believe, do not give practical guidelines to building and using existing expert systems technology. This book, however, does present useful guidelines, and future knowledge engineers will learn from the experiences of the author and others discussed in the text.

Where this Book Could Be Used

At the college level, this book could be used for a business, engineering, or computer science course on "Introduction to Expert Systems," "Applied Expert Systems," or "Building Expert Systems." The book is also appropriate for a continuing education or extension course throughout higher education. In any of these situations, the book could be a primary or supplementary text.

Organization

This book discusses the expert system life cycle development steps, from problem selection to implementation. To reinforce the life cycle approach, a case study on READ is presented and used throughout the book. READ is an expert system prototype developed to determine software functional requirements for command management activities of NASA supported satellites. It was developed by using KES (Knowledge Engineering System), an expert system shell by Software Architecture & Engineering. Newer and more powerful versions of KES now exist than the version shown in this book. Another expert system prototype, a business-oriented case study, is discussed in Appendix C. A glossary of expert system/artificial intelligence terms is provided for the reader at the back of the book. Additionally, extensive references are provided at the end of each chapter.

Acknowledgments

I would like to thank Barry Silverman, Sam Rothman, Homer Sewell, Thomas Nagy, James Dinwiddie, Robert Waters, Ernest Forman, John Carson, and Donald Gross for their kind advice. Many thanks are due to Patricia Lightfoot, Peter Kurzhals, Thomas Grenchik, Randy Shumaker, Jude Franklin, James Slagle, Laura Davis, Yi-Tzuu Chien, J. W. Perkins, Chip Blouin, Dan DeSalvo, Nancy Goodman, Bob Dutilly, and Thomas Pfarr for their helpful assistance. Great appreciation is due to Andrew Ferrantino at Software Architecture & Engineering, Inc., Decision Support Software, Inc., Dean Norma Loeser, Erik Winslow, Barbara Greenall, Dorothy Seidman, and Rita Hodge. I also give special thanks to my wife, Janet, for all her help, and my parents and family for allowing me the opportunity to gain and appreciate an education. I greatly appreciate the many reviewers' comments, and especially thank Raleigh Wilson, Cecelia Morales, Greg Hubit, and Mitchell Publishing for their kind advice during preparation of this manuscript.

For their perceptive reviews on the original and revised manuscript, I'd like to thank: Lance B. Eliot, University of Southern California; Perry Sanders, Roosevelt University; John Turcheck, Robert Morris College; Jack Phillip, Roosevelt University; and A. Terry Bahill, University of Arizona.

The views expressed in this book do not necessarily reflect the views of those at NASA Goddard Space Flight Center.

Jay Liebowitz, D.Sc.
Washington, D.C.

1 Overview of Expert Systems

First there were databases and database management systems. Then information bases developed, whereby management information systems and decision support systems sprouted. Now there are knowledge bases on which expert systems are being built. The age of knowledge is upon us, and computer programs are being developed to preserve this knowledge. These computer programs are **expert systems** that mimic the behavior of human experts in some specified domain of knowledge. The area of expert systems is gaining worldwide interest in industry, government, and academia. From telephone cable maintenance to medical diagnosis to tax planning, expert systems are being used for an increasing number of applications. Expert systems is a subset of artificial intelligence and draws upon many disciplines, including cognitive psychology, linguistics, philosophy, and computer science. Although more research is needed to improve expert systems technology, expert systems are beginning to have a strong impact on assisting in the decision making process.

Artificial intelligence promises us computers that can reason, learn, and understand. This ambitious goal is moving toward fruition with such worldwide efforts as Japan's Fifth Generation Project, the United States' Strategic Computing Project, and Europe's consortium, ESPRIT. A major goal is to produce a **fifth generation** computer capable of understanding in natural language, able to recognize and produce speech, and having the ability to reason and learn. If this goal is realized by the 1990s—although numerous people feel this date is very optimistic—what can we look forward to in this age of artificial intelligence?

To answer this question, let's take a look at a typical situation that might be commonplace in the mid to late 1990s, assuming artificial intelligence has penetrated the marketplace and home.

▐ A Situation at Home in 1999

Mom comes home after working as an attorney, putting in the extra billable hours required of all associates. She calls for her son, Joey, and he doesn't answer.

Dad calls out from his study that Joey is playing in the park with his friends. Mom checks her watch and realizes it is almost 7:15 p.m., and Joey really should be home. She presses a button on her watch and then types in a message on her watch: "Come home for dinner."

Joey, playing friskily in the park, hears a beeping sound on his watch, and across the face of it sees this message flashing: "Come home for dinner." Joey pushes a button on his watch, which is preprogrammed to dial home. Joey then talks into his speech-recognizable watch and tells Mom that he'll be home in 10 minutes. Mom talks into her watch and tells Joey to hurry home.

After speaking to Joey, Mom slouches back into her chair to rest from an exhausting day of litigation and legal research. The only savior of the day was using a natural language interface to the legal retrieval system for doing the legal research, instead of having to worry about the correct keywords and their combinations to search for cases.

Dad comes out of his study and asks what Mom would like for dinner, since it's Dad's turn to cook tonight. Mom says, "How about putting in the chicken that I bought yesterday?"

Dad replies, "Okay." He then washes the chicken and puts the four breasts into the oven. He presses a button which reads, "Chicken," and then a question appears on the oven's control board. It asks if it is a roast of chicken or pieces. Dad hits the button for pieces, and another message appears on the control board—"What kind of pieces and how many?" Dad hits the entry for breasts and then hits the number four. A message appears on the control board, "The chicken will be cooked at 350 degrees and will be done in 40 minutes." Then the oven turns on at 350 degrees, and Dad sits back and gloats about these new knowledge-based ovens, which make cooking easy even for him.

All of a sudden, Joey comes in through the side door and yells, "Hi, I'm home." He rushes over to Mom and Dad and recounts his day in the park. As Joey is explaining his day's events, Mom notices that Joey has some rash on his arms and neck. Mom asks Joey, "How long have you had the rash? Does it hurt?"

Joey replies, "I just noticed it when I was coming home from the park. It really itches."

Mom goes to the PC on the side of the kitchen counter and loads an expert system to help diagnose common medical problems. The expert system tells her that Joey has a 95% chance of having poison ivy and he should put on calamine lotion. The expert system also indicates that there is a 5% chance of a heat rash, and the family doctor should be consulted in either case. Mom decides to put calamine lotion on tonight and then makes an appointment via electronic mail to see the doctor tomorrow.

A bell rings and Dad yells out from the kitchen, "Dinner time." A robot, adeptly and carefully carrying a tray of chicken and vegetables, passes Mom and Joey on the way to the dinner table. The robot then stops at the table and raises its arms so the tray is level with the table. It pushes its arms onto the table so the food can be positioned on the table. It then releases the tray with the food onto the table, pulls back its arms, puts them to the side, turns around, and heads back into the kitchen.

After eating a delicious dinner, the family lets the robot load the dishwasher, and Mom and Joey go into the family room to watch TV. Dad goes back into his study to finish his lecture for tomorrow's class. He leans back in his chair and says, "This would not have been possible without artificial intelligence." As soon as he starts to talk, a typewriter types out his dictation. Without Dad even lifting a finger, the typewriter types out his lecture, using his words, and even correcting any grammatical errors. Dad sits back, with the TV in the background, and thinks, "What a life!"

Be Ready

The situation just presented is not far-fetched. Already, a company is developing a "Dick Tracy–type" wristwatch to be test marketed in 1989. Another company has developed a typewriter with a 10,000-word vocabulary that can almost simultaneously type out what an individual is dictating. Expert systems are being developed and sold already to help the layperson perform some simple, routine functions such as preparing a will or drafting a contract. Robots for use in the home have been developed to carry a newspaper or a drink, and even to walk the dog. Microwave ovens are becoming more sophisticated by having more features available to the user at simply the press of a button.

So the scenario previously discussed is possible in the years to come in terms of technical achievement. One application of artificial intelligence, presented in this scenario, that is gaining worldwide attention is expert systems. Expert systems are being used for such far-ranging applications as diagnosing mechanical problems in locomotives, determining whether credit card fraud exists, and performing personal and corporate financial planning. The Gartner Group [24] estimates that U.S. sales of expert systems will hit $300 million by 1992, up from $25 million in 1987. The U.S. market for artificial intelligence gear is expected to be as much as $1 billion in 1992.

This chapter presents an overview of expert systems technology, highlighting certain areas. Subsequent chapters will amplify each of these areas.

Definition

An expert system is a computer program that emulates the behavior of human experts within a specific domain of knowledge. Expert systems are particularly relevant for inferring and deducing from problems involving unstructured aspects [15]. They constitute a structured methodology for conduct of analogical investigation. The major characteristics of an expert system include:

1. the ability to perform at the level of an expert;

2. representation of domain-specific knowledge in the manner in which the expert thinks;

3. incorporation of explanation processes and ways of handling uncertainty; and

4. typically, pertinence to problems that can be symbolically represented.

An expert system differs from a conventional computer program mainly by being more tolerant of errors and imperfect knowledge, and by separating the expert knowledge from the general-reasoning mechanism. By having this partitioning of the **knowledge base** from the control structure, the knowledge base can be incrementally developed, and the same general system can be used for different applications by "removing" the knowledge base and "inserting" another.

In the past, expert systems have worked well in problem areas with ill and unstructured aspects, as shown by the following characteristics:

- There existed at least one expert in the problem area who is generally acknowledged as such.
- The sources of the expert's expertise were judgment and experience.
- The problem was well-bounded to prevent an unmanageably large search space.
- The problem area had a real consensus—not, for example, like macroeconomic policy.
- Test data was easily available.

Background of Expert Systems

Lord Kelvin once characterized scientific knowledge this way:

> When you can measure what you are speaking about, and express it in numbers, you know something about it; but when you cannot measure it, when you cannot express it in numbers, your knowledge is of a meager and unsatisfactory kind: it may be the beginning of knowledge, but you have scarcely, in your thoughts, advanced to a stage of *science*. [1]

This quote stresses the need for having quantitative descriptions of natural phenomena. The field of artificial intelligence, of which expert systems are a part, developed to encompass the *symbolic* nature and subjective qualities of phenomena, rather than the numerical operations. Many natural phenomena, like planning and problem-solving, are difficult to represent numerically. From Lord Kelvin's observation and the subsequent realization that digital computers are general-purpose processors of symbols, the field of artificial intelligence emerged.

Two main schools of thought relate to artificial intelligence. Michie [2] associates one with those who work toward the construction of intelligent artifacts, or seek to uncover principles, methods, and techniques useful in such construction, and the other with those who view information-processing models of human thought.

The largest school is by far the first group. Early work in this group looked for simple, general, and powerful reasoning techniques, such as the General Problem Solver by Newell, Shaw, and Simon. Unfortunately, these general methods were unsuccessful in solving larger and more complicated real-world problems due to their being unable to cope with the enormous number of alternatives. It was then recognized that knowledge was as important as logical reasoning, and methods for representing and using knowledge emerged. Out of this effort the formulation of expert systems began.

Emerging from the two aforementioned varying schools of thought is the spectrum of artificial intelligence (AI). The WHAT end of the spectrum involves *what* the user wishes the computer, as his/her instrument, to do. The HOW end involves the user supplying intelligence to instruct the machine, with precision, on exactly *how* to do the job, step-by-step. The long-range goal of AI is the WHAT end.

Expert systems are closest to the HOW end of the spectrum, but are slowly approaching the WHAT end. Humans often solve a problem by finding a way of thinking about it that makes the solution easy. According to Barr and Feigenbaum [3], expert systems, so far, must be told *how* to think about the problems they solve (i.e., the space in which to search for the solution).

The early work in expert systems began in the 1950s with the Rand-Carnegie team of Newell, Shaw, and Simon. They developed the General Problem Solver (GPS) to solve problems of elementary logic, chess, and high school algebra word problems. Besides the Rand-Carnegie team, the MIT Group of Minsky and McCarthy was instrumental in the late 1950s and early 1960s in building a foundation for expert systems. McCarthy invented **LISP** programming language, which is the dominant language used in artificial intelligence and expert systems. Also in the 1960s, Lederberg, Buchanan, and Feigenbaum began to develop an expert system called DENDRAL, which would infer a structure of molecules by mass spectography data. Other work on expert systems in the 1960s included SAINT (Slagle, 1961) for symbolic integration, STUDENT (Bobrow) for solving high school algebra word problems, and an expert system by Raphael for question-answering using trivial databases.

The 1970s saw greater industrial interest in developing expert systems—an interest that continues through today. Expert systems are being developed in application areas such as diagnosis, perception, instruction, learning, game playing, programming, theorem proving, and pattern and speech recognition.

Industrial interest has been shown by Digital Equipment, Texas Instruments, Xerox, Schlumberger, Hewlett-Packard, General Motors, IBM, and others. Universities, such as Stanford, Carnegie-Mellon, Rutgers, Maryland, and MIT, continue to pursue expert system technology. Universities and private companies have been instrumental in developing other programming languages used in expert systems like Interlisp, MacLisp, IQLisp, Franz Lisp, PROLOG, OPS5, PLANNER, and UNITS.

Through applying AI ideas to expert systems over the years, two major insights have been learned [2]. The first insight is that "knowledge-rich" is essential for an expert system to work successfully, even if it is "methods-poor." The second insight derived through working with expert systems is that a specialist's knowledge is largely **heuristic**—experiential and uncertain. Therefore, an expert system must have corrections for uncertainty, and **explanation** must be built into the system so the person using the system can understand how the conclusions have been derived.

Components of Expert Systems

An expert system consists of three major components:

1. dialog structure,
2. inference engine, and
3. knowledge base.

Dialog Structure

The **dialog structure** serves as the language interface in which the user can access the expert system. Usually, the user interacts with the expert system via a consultative mode. An explanation module is also included in the expert system. The explanation module allows the user to challenge the expert system and examine its reasoning process. Michie [4] identifies three different user-modes for an expert system:

1. getting answers to problems—user as client;

2. improving or increasing the system's knowledge—user as tutor; and

3. harvesting the knowledge base for human use—user as pupil.

Each of these three modes requires interaction through the dialog structure.

▌ Inference Engine

The second component of an expert system is the **inference engine**, a program that allows hypotheses to be generated from the information in the knowledge base.

Three major methods incorporated into the inference engine allow it efficiently to **search** a space for deriving hypotheses from the knowledge base. These solution-direction techniques are forward chaining, backward chaining, and forward and backward processing combined. **Forward chaining**, often described as **event-driven**, or **data-driven** reasoning, is used for problem solving when data or basic ideas are a starting point. Under this method the system does not start with any particular defined goals. One possible drawback of forward chaining is that one would derive everything possible whether one needed it or not. Forward chaining has been used in expert systems for data analysis, design, diagnosis, and concept formation.

Backward chaining, called **goal-driven** reasoning, entails having a goal or a hypothesis as a starting point, and then "working backwards" along some paths to see if the conclusion is true. A problem with backward chaining is that the combining of sub-goals could lead to a problem where an explosion of combinations of possibilities could result. Expert systems using backward chaining are used for diagnosis and planning.

Forward and backward processing combined, another method for generating hypotheses to produce the solution, is used for searching a large area, so both a bottom-up and top-down search can be appropriately combined. This combined search is applicable to complex problems incorporating uncertainties, such as speech understanding.

Besides these three approaches, techniques can be built into the inference engine to search a large space and to transform the search space. Some of these methods are described in the works of Gevarter [5], Stefik et al. [6], and Winston et al. [7], as well as in Chapter 5:

- Exhaustive Search
- Generate and Test
- Guessing or Plausible Reasoning
- Relevant Backtracking
- Least Commitment
- Multilines of Reasoning
- Multiple Models
- Break into Subproblems
- Hierarchical Refinement
- Hierarchical Resolution
- Meta Rules

Inference engines have some capabilities for the aforementioned search space approaches, and most of them also have the ability for reasoning in the presence of uncertainty. In many cases one must deal with uncertainty in data or in knowledge. Thus an expert system should allow for handling this uncertainty, as discussed later in the chapter.

Knowledge Base

The knowledge base, the most important component of an expert system, is comprised of **domain knowledge**—facts and rules of thumb based upon experience. According to Duda [8], the most powerful expert systems are the ones containing the most knowledge.

There are four major ways to represent knowledge in the knowledge base. The first technique is by means of formulas in **first-order predicate calculus**. Predicate calculus, a system of formal logic based on determining whether a given proposition is true or false, allows relationships between these propositions to be specified and generalizations to be made.

The second approach to representing knowledge is the use of **frames** as developed by Marvin Minsky in 1975. Frames are data structures in which all knowledge about a particular object is stored together. Frames are used for declarative knowledge, which is more descriptive than procedural. They use a slot-and-filler technique, where data or information is manipulated within the slots and among the frames via procedural attachments, such as if-added or if-needed procedures. A special kind of frame is a **script** that allows various scenes to be represented in a frame-like orientation.

Closely aligned with the frames concept is the use of **semantic** or associative **networks**. According to Nau [9], this method organizes knowledge around the objects being described, but here the objects are represented by **nodes** in a graph, and the relations among them are represented by labeled arcs. The main advantage of semantic networks over logical representation (like predicate calculus) is that, for each object, all the relevant information is collected together.

The last major technique of representing knowledge in the knowledge base is the use of **production rules**. Production rules were popularized by Newell and Simon in 1972 and by Davis and King in 1975. Production rules take the form of IF (**antecedent** or **condition**) THEN (**consequent** or **conclusion**), or SITUATION-ACTION. They have been used extensively in expert systems, particularly for diagnosis and planning.

It should be recognized, however, that a principal refinement for expert systems continues to be the need for effective filtering out of the knowledge base biases that are imparted by the particular, unique views and values [15] of the experts who are the sources of the knowledge that constitute knowledge bases.

Building an Expert System

The time for construction of early expert systems was in the range of 20 to 50 person-years. Recently, simple expert systems can be built in 3 person-months, but a complex system is still apt to take as long as 10 person-years to complete. With the previously mentioned search-space strategies and appropriate expert system shells (discussed later), development time is approaching 5 person-years per system.

The first step in building an expert system is to select the problem, define the expert system goal(s), and identify the sources of knowledge. The task must have a well-bounded **domain** of application—typically, the task should take a few hours to a few weeks to solve. Additionally, there must be at least one willing expert for developing the expert system.

Once this step is accomplished, the next procedure is to acquire the knowledge from the **domain expert** to develop the knowledge base. It is also helpful to develop a framework for representing the acquired information. **Knowledge acquisition** is an iterative process in which many meetings with the expert are needed to gather all the relevant and necessary information for the knowledge base.

After the knowledge is acquired, the next step is to select a **knowledge representation** approach. These approaches include using predicate calculus, frames, semantic networks, or production rules, as described in the previous section. According to Software Architecture & Engineering, Inc. [10,11], rule-based deduction would be an appropriate method to use for knowledge representation if:

1. the underlying knowledge is already organized as rules;

2. the type of classification is predominantly categorical; and

3. there is not a large amount of context-dependence.

Frames or semantic networks are best used when the knowledge pre-exists as descriptions.

The next step deals with **knowledge programming** by using a text editor in an expert system shell or by using LISP, PROLOG, or some other appropriate programming language. Then the last step can be achieved by validating, testing, and evaluating the expert system.

Validity assessment is necessary to check the knowledge base and the expert system as a whole. Validity can be achieved by running the knowledge base on past problems. Validity can also be confirmed by other experts knowledgeable in the problem domain.

Testing is an important area to be examined because when the expert system finally runs, it typically produces a variety of unexpected results. These unexpected results are summarized by Hayes-Roth et al. [12]:

- Excess generality—special cases overlooked.
- Excess specificity—generality undetected.
- Concept poverty—useful relationship not detected and exploited.
- Invalid knowledge—misstatement of facts or approximations.
- Ambiguous knowledge—implicit dependencies not adequately articulated.
- Invalid reasoning—programmer incorrectly transforms knowledge.
- Inadequate integration—dependencies among multiple pieces of advice incompletely integrated.
- Limited horizon—consequences of recent, past, or probable future events not exploited.
- Egocentricity—little attention paid to probable meaning of others' actions.

To correct these bugs, knowledge refinement and maintenance must be accomplished.

After knowledge refinement and maintenance are achieved, an evaluation of the expert system can be made by users currently working in the problem domain. This evaluation process is a postaudit to see if the expert system meets the objectives for which it was developed.

Expert System Shells

As previously mentioned, building an expert system from scratch could take more than 20 person-years. To decrease development time and associated costs, many expert systems are developed by using an **expert system shell**. An expert system shell contains a generalized dialog structure and inference engine. A knowledge base can be designed for a specific problem domain, and it would be linked to the expert system shell to form a new expert system for a particular application.

There are many expert system shells, including these:

ROSIE	Rand Corporation
AGE	Stanford University
HEARSAY III	U.S.C./Information Sciences Institute
EMYCIN	Stanford University
Exsys	Exsys, Inc.
RAINBOW	IBM
KMS/KES and	University of Maryland/Software
SPECTRUM	Architecture & Engineering, Inc.
EXPERT	Rutgers University
ARBY	Smart Systems
MECS-AI	Tokyo University
KAS	SRI
TEIRESIAS	Stanford University
M.1/S.1	Teknowledge Inc.
Expert Ease	Jeffrey Perrone & Associates/Human Edge
ART	Inference Corporation
TIMM	General Research Corporation
INSIGHT and INSIGHT 2	Level 5 Corporation
KEE	Intellicorp
Personal Consultant and	Texas Instruments
Personal Consultant Plus	
SRL+ and Knowledge Craft	Carnegie Group
PLUME	Carnegie Group
REVEAL	Infotym
PICON	LISP Machines Inc.
DUCK	Smart Systems
Rulemaster	Radian Corporation
KDS	KDS Corporation
GoldWorks	Gold Hill Computers
Guru	Micro Database Systems
VP-Expert	Paperback Software

Explanation, Uncertainty, and Human Factors Considerations

Ways of handling explanation, uncertainty, and ergonomics are important features to be incorporated into an expert system. Explanation capabilities are needed so that the user can question and challenge the results from the expert system as well as understand how the results were achieved. In MYCIN, an expert system designed to diagnose bacterial infections in the blood, explanation can be arrived at as shown below, with the user asking the questions [13]:

```
1. **HOW DID YOU DECIDE THAT ORGANISM-1 MIGHT BE AN E.COLI?
     I used RULE021 to conclude that the identity of ORGANISM-1
is e.coli. This gave a cumulative CF of (.47).
     Then I used RULE084 to conclude that the identity of
ORGANISM-1 is e.coli. This gave a cumulative CF of (.55).
     Finally, I used RULE033 to conclude that the identity of
ORGANISM-1 is e.coli. This gave a cumulative CF of (.74).
2. **DID YOU USE RULE163 TO FIND OUT ANYTHING ABOUT ORGANISM-1?
     RULE163 was tried in the context of ORGANISM-1 but it
failed because it is not true that the patient has had a
genito-urinary tract manipulative procedure (clause 3).
3. **DID RULE116 TELL YOU ANYTHING ABOUT INFECTION-1?
     No. RULE116 would be relevant to the primary-bacteremia
when applied to ORGANISM-1.
     But clause 2 ("the gram stain of the organism is not
known") was already known to be false for ORGANISM-1, so the
rule was never tried.
4. **WHY DIDN'T YOU CONSIDER STREPTOCOCCUS AS A POSSIBILITY FOR
ORGANISM-1?
     The following rule could have been used to determine that
the identity of ORGANISM-1 was streptococcus: RULE033
     But clause 2 ("the morphology if the organism is coccus")
was already known to be false for ORGANISM-1, so the rule was
never tried.
```

Besides explanation capabilities, uncertainty and human factors should also be incorporated into the expert system. Even the expert is not sure 100% of the time; thus, an expert system should handle uncertainty. Several ways of handling uncertainty include Bayesian statistics, belief functions (Dempster-Shafer Method and certainty factors), and fuzzy set theory. Human factors should also be designed into expert systems. Some possible features are the use of messages, menus, free-text attachments, rules against undesirable input, and high-level English-like representation language for encoding the knowledge. With these considerations built into the design of the expert system, the system's success will be greatly enhanced.

Applications of Expert Systems

Businesses and universities in the U.S. and abroad are becoming increasingly active in the development of expert systems. Japan launched a fifth generation computer project in April 1982 whose goal was to surpass the United States in expert system technology over a 10-year horizon. The projected budget was approximately $800 million to develop and implement ideas in knowledge-based engineering, problem solving and inference systems, intelligent interfaces, and logic processing machines.

In the United States, the federal government has been the principal source of funds for work in expert systems. The government agencies most actively involved are the Defense Advanced Research Projects Agency, National Institutes of Health, National Science Foundation, Office of Naval Research, National Library of Medicine, Air Force Offices of Scientific Research, U.S. Geological Survey, Navy Center for Applied Research in Artificial Intelligence, and the National Aeronautics and Space Administration.

Besides the government, universities and companies are showing an active interest in expert systems. Stanford, MIT, and Carnegie-Mellon are some of the leaders in expert systems development among the universities. The following companies are examples of those engaged in expert systems development: SRI, RAND, MITRE, ADS, AMOCO, BBN, Bell Labs, Computer Thought, DEC, Fairchild, GM, Hewlett-Packard, Hughes, IBM, Intellicorp, JAYCOR, Machine Intelligence Corp., Martin Marietta, Schlumberger, Smart Systems Technology, Systems Control Inc., Texas Instruments, Teknowledge, TRW, and XEROX.

Most of the existing expert systems fall under the functions of diagnosis, data analysis, planning, design, analysis, concept formation, monitoring, knowledge acquisition, computer-aided instruction, tutoring, management, automatic programming, or image understanding.

Some existing expert systems are listed below [16–18], but many of these are either in the research or field prototype stages.

DIAGNOSIS

PIP	Massachusetts Institute of Technology (MIT)
CASNET	Rutgers University
INTERNIST and CADUCEUS	University of Pittsburgh
MYCIN	Stanford University
PUFF	Stanford University
DART	Stanford University
MDX	Ohio State University
IDT	Digital Equipment Corporation (DEC)
REACTOR	EG&G Idaho
IN-ATE	Automated Reasoning Corporation
DELTA	General Electric
GEN-X	General Electric
COMPASS	GTE Labs
ACE	Bell Labs
NEMESYS	Bell Labs
YES/MVS	IBM

ANALYSIS

DIPMETER ADVISOR	MIT/Schlumberger
DENDRAL	Stanford University
GA1	Stanford University

PROSPECTOR	SRI
CRYSALIS	Stanford University
RX	Stanford University
ABEL	MIT
ELAS	AMOCO
EL	MIT
MECHO	University of Edinburgh
TECH	RAND CORP
SPERIL	Purdue University
CRITTER	Rutgers University
EDASS	Booz, Allen & Hamilton
LDS	Rand Corporation
EVIDENT	George Washington University
READ	George Washington University
SACON	Stanford University
TAXADVISOR	University of Illinois
MANAGEMENT ADVISOR	Palladian
PLANPOWER	Applied Expert Systems
FOLIO	Stanford University
EXPERTAX	Coopers & Lybrand
AY/ASQ	Arthur Young
AUTHORIZER'S ASST.	American Express
MORTGAGE LOAN AUTHORIZER	Arthur Andersen
AUDITOR	University of Illinois
CASH VALUE	Heuros Lts.
PERSONAL FINANCIAL PLANNER	Arthur D. Little
TRADER'S ASSISTANT	Arthur D. Little
TICOM	University of Minnesota
EDP AUDITOR	Brigham Young University and University of Florida
CONCEPT	Tymshare

DESIGN

R1/XCON	DEC
SYN	MIT
SYNCHEM	State University of New York–Stonybrook

PLANNING

SACHS	University of California at Santa Cruz
NOAH	SRI
ABSTRIPS	SRI
DEVISER	Jet Propulsion Lab
OP-PLANNER	Rand
MOLGEN	Stanford University

KNOBS	MITRE Corporation
ISIS	Carnegie Mellon University (CMU)
SPEX	Stanford University
HODGKINS	MIT
RBMS	Ford Aerospace & Communications
NAVEX	Inference Corporation
ERS	PAR Technology
FAITH	Jet Propulsion Lab

LEARN FROM EXPERIENCE

METADENDRAL	Stanford University
EURISKO	Stanford University/MCC
AM	Stanford University
TEIRESIAS	Stanford University

MONITORING

VM	Stanford University

COMPUTER-AIDED INSTRUCTION

SOPHIE	Bolt, Beranek & Newman (BNN)
GUIDON	Stanford University
EXCHECK	Stanford University
STEAMER	BNN
BUGGY	BNN
WHY	BNN
WEST	BNN
WUMPUS	MIT
SCHOLAR	BNN

INTELLIGENT ASSISTANT

BATTLE	Navy Center for Applied Research in AI
DIGITALIS THERAPY ADVISOR	MIT
RAYDEX	Rutgers
XSEL	CMU/DEC
ONCOCIN	Stanford University
CSA	Georgia Tech
RECONSIDER	University of California at San Francisco

MANAGEMENT

IMS	CMU
CALLISTO	DEC
KRT	McDonnell Douglas

AUTOMATIC PROGRAMMING

PHOENIX	Schlumberger Doll

CHI	Kestrel Institute
PECOS	Stanford University
LIBRA	Stanford University
SAFE	University of Southern California
DEDALUS	SRI
PROGRAMMER'S APPRENTICE	MIT

IMAGE UNDERSTANDING

VISIONS	University of Massachusetts at Amherst
ACRONYM	Stanford University
ANALYST	MITRE Corp.
HASP/SIAP	Stanford University

Figures 1-1 through 1-5 show sample user sessions of five expert systems: MYCIN [13], XCON [21], SOPHIE [22], TAXADVISOR [23], and BATTLE [24]. MYCIN diagnoses bacterial infections in the blood; XCON is used to configure VAX computers; SOPHIE is used for computer-aided instruction of electronics; TAXADVISOR is used to provide estate planning tax advice; and BATTLE is designed for weapon-target resource allocation problems.

Figure 1-1

Sample user session with MYCIN

```
----------------------------------------PATIENT-1----------------------------------------
(1) Patient's name:(first-last)
**FRED SMITH

(2) Sex:
**MALE

(3) Age:
**55

(4)Have you been able to obtain positive cultures from a site at which Fred Smith
has an infection?
**YES

        ---------------------------------INFECTION-1---------------------------------
        (5) What is the infection?
        **PRIMARY-BACTEREMIA

        (6) Please give the date and approximate time when signs or symptoms of
        the primary-bacteremia (INFECTION-1) first appeared. (mo/da/yr)
        **MAY 5, 1975

The most recent positive culture associated with the primary-bacteremia
(INFECTION-1) will be referred to as:
```

Figure 1-1

(continued)

```
-------------------------------------CULTURE-1------------------------------------
        (7) From what site was the specimen for CULTURE-1 taken?
        **BLOOD


                                    .
                                    .
                                    .

My therapy recommendation will be based on the following probable infection(s)
and potential causative organism(s):

INFECTION-1 is PRIMARY-BACTEREMIA

                                                         {Possible identities}

<Item 1> The identity of ORGANISM-1 may be PSEUDOMONAS-AERUGINOSA
<Item 2> The identity of ORGANISM-1 may be KLEBSIELLA-PNEUMONIAE
<Item 3> The identity of ORGANISM-1 may be E. COLI
<Item 4> The identity of ORGANISM-1 may be BACTEROIDES-FRAGILIS
<Item 5> The identity of ORGANISM-1 may be ENTEROBACTER
<Item 6> The identity of ORGANISM-1 may be PROTEUS-NON-MIRABILIS


(46) On a scale of 0 to 4, where higher numbers indicate increasing severity, how
would you rate Fred Smith's degree of sickness?
**3


(47) Does Fred Smith have a clinically significant allergic reaction to any
antimicrobal agent?
**NO


(48) Fred Smith's weight in kilograms (or <number> POUNDS):
**70

                            {note that 2 drugs cover for 6 potential organisms}
[Rec 1] My preferred therapy recommendation is as follows:
In order to cover for Items <1 2 3 5 6>:
     Give: GENTAMICIN
     Dose: 119 mg (1.7 mg/kg) q8h IV [or IM] for 10 days
     Comments: Modify dose in renal failure
In order to cover for Item <4>:
     Give: CLINDAMYCIN
     Dose: 595 mg (8.5 mg/kg) q6h IV [or IM] for 14 days
     Comments: If diarrhea or other GI symptoms develop, patient should be
     evaluated for possible pseudomembranous colitis.

Do you wish to see the next choice therapy?

                                          {alternative choices are available}
**Y


Which, if any, of the above drugs do you wish eliminated from consideration?
**CLINDAMYCIN

[Rec 2] Next best therapy recommendation:
In order to cover for Items <2 3 4 5 6>:
     Give: CHLORAMPHENICOL
     Dose: 1 gm (15 mg/kg) q6h IV for 14 days
     Comments: Monitor patient's white count
```

Figure 1-1

(continued)

```
In order to cover for Item <1>:
     Give: GENTAMICIN
     Dose: 119 mg (1.7mg/kg) q8h IV [or IM] for 10 days
     Comments: Modify dose in renal failure
```

Source: Davis, R., B. Buchanan, and E. Shortliffe. "Production Rules as a Representation for a Knowledge-Based Consultation System." *Artificial Intelligence*, Vol. 8, No. 1, North-Holland (1977). Reprinted with permission from North-Holland Publishing Company, Amsterdam.

Figure 1-2

Sample user session with R1/XCON

```
COMPONENTS ORDERED:
1 SV-AXHHA-LA  [packaged system]
1 FP780-AA     [floating point accelerator]
1 DW780-AA     [unibus adaptor]
1 BA11-KE      [unibus expansion cabinet box]
6 MS780-DC     [memory]
1 MS780-CA     [memory controller]
1 H9602-HA     [cpu expansion cabinet]
1 H7111-A      [clock battery backup]
1 H7112-A      [memory battery backup]
1 REP05-AA     [single port disk drive]
4 RP05-BA      [dual port disk drive]
1 TEE16-AE     [tape drive with formatter]
2 TEI6-AE      [tape drive]
8 RK07-EA      [single port disk drive]
1 DR11-B       [direct memory access interface]
1 LP11-CA      [line printer]
1 DZ11-F       [multiplexer with panel]
1 DZ11-B       [multiplexer]
2 LA-36-CE     [hard copy terminal]
```

This is the result of R1's analysis.

```
SUBSTITUTIONS
NONE

                         COMPONENTS ADDED
                         1 H7101
                         1 M9014
                         1 M9202
                         1 M9302
                         1 070-11528

THE FOLLOWING COMPONENTS WERE NOT CONFIGURED
   2 RK07-EA*        (POSSIBLY-FORGOTTEN-PREREQUISITE
                      DISK-DRIVE CONTROLLER)
   1 H7111-A         (NOT-NEEDED)
   1 H7100-A         (NOT-NEEDED)
   6 BC06R-10        (NOT-NEEDED)
   2 070-12292108    (NOT-NEEDED)
   1 BC05F-15        (NOT-NEEDED)
   2 BC11A-10        (NOT-NEEDED)
```

Figure 1-2

(continued)

```
POSSIBLY FORGOTTEN COMPONENTS
3 BCO5L-15 TO CONNECT UBA O TO BOX 1 OF CABINET 1
1 RK611* TO SUPPORT 2 UNUSED DISK-DRIVES

UNUSED CAPACITY
THE MEMORY CONTROLLER (MS780-CA*) IN THE CPUX
    CABINET COULD SUPPORT 768 K BYTES MORE MEMORY
THE MEMORY CONTROLLER (MS780-CA*) IN THE CPU
    CABINET COULD SUPPORT 768 K BYTES MORE MEMORY
DZ11-D* 1 IN BOX 2 OF CABINET 1 COULD SUPPORT 7 MORE
    MA20 LINES (THROUGH PANEL 2)
DZ11-D* 2 IN BOX 2 OF CABINET 1 COULD SUPPORT 7 MORE
    MA20 LINES (THROUGH PANEL 2)
DZ11-B* 2 IN BOX 1 OF CABINET 1 IS UNUSED (IT CAN SUP-
    PORT 8 EIA LINES (THROUGH PANEL 1))
DZ11-B* 1 IN BOX 1 OF CABINET 1 IS UNUSED (IT CAN SUP-
    PORT 8 EIA LINES (THROUGH PANEL 1))
MBA O COULD SUPPORT 2 MORE MB-DEVICES AND ITS 1 MAS-
    TER TAPE DRIVES COULD SUPPORT 5 MORE SLAVES
MBA 1 COULD SUPPORT 4 MORE MB-DEVICES
                            .
                            .
                            .
```

R1 next displays a series of drawings that indicate how the various machine components may be assembled and configured in the working computer system.

Source:

Weiss, Sholom M. and Casimir A. Kulikowski, *A Practical Guide to Designing Expert Systems* (Totowa, NJ: Rowman & Allanheld, 1984), pp. 61–63. Reprinted with permission from Rowman & Allanheld, Totowa, New Jersey.

Figure 1-3

Sample user session with SOPHIE

```
SOPHIE: The power supply is broken.  The current front panel
switch settings are as follows . . .
STUDENT: What is the output voltage?
SOPHIE: The output voltage is 11.7 volts.
STUDENT: What is it in a working power supply?
SOPHIE: 19.9 volts.
STUDENT: What is the voltage between R8 and Q1?
SOPHIE: 47.6 volts.
STUDENT: Replace Q6.
SOPHIE: How do you think Q6 is faulty? Is it shorted?
STUDENT: No.
SOPHIE: Is Q6 an open circuit?
STUDENT: I think so.
SOPHIE: Q6 is not faulted in that manner.
STUDENT: Was it possible that Q6 was an open circuit?
SOPHIE: Yes, that fault is consistent with all of the
        measurements you have made.
```

Source:

Brown, J. S., and R. J. Bobrow. *Applications of Artificial Intelligence Techniques in Maintenance Training. New Concepts in Maintenance Training and Performance Aids.* Report NAVTRAEQUIPCEN IH–255 (October 1975).

Figure 1-4

*Sample user session
with TAXADVISOR*

<u>TAXADVISOR DIALOG ON MAKING PERMANENT GIFTS</u>

```
1)   DOES THE CLIENT HAVE AN ESTATE THAT IS SUBSTANTIAL ENOUGH,
     GIVEN HIS PRESENT AGE AND HEALTH, THAT HE CAN AFFORD TO
     FOREGO THE INCOME FROM GIFTED ASSETS AND PAY THE
     EXPENSES ASSOCIATED WITH MAKING GIFTS?
**   Y


2)   IS THE CLIENT WILLING TO RELINQUISH POSSESSION AND
     ENJOYMENT OF ASSETS AND POWER TO ALTER, AMEND, REVOKE, OR
     TERMINATE ANY TRUST IN WHICH THE ASSETS ARE PLACED?
**WHY
THIS WILL AID IN DETERMINING WHETHER THE CLIENT SHOULD MAKE
PERMANENT GIFTS.  IT HAS ALREADY BEEN ESTABLISHED THAT
          CLIENT HAS AN ESTATE THAT IS SUBSTANTIAL ENOUGH,
          GIVEN HIS PRESENT AGE AND HEALTH, THAT HE CAN
          AFFORD TO FOREGO THE INCOME FROM GIFTED ASSETS AND
          PAY THE EXPENSES ASSOCIATED WITH MAKING GIFTS.
THEREFORE, IF
1.   A:   CLIENT IS WILLING TO RELINQUISH POSSESSION AND
          ENJOYMENT OF ASSETS AND POWER TO ALTER, AMEND, REVOKE,
          OR TERMINATE ANY TRUST IN WHICH THE ASSETS ARE PLACED,
          OR
     B:   IS WILLING TO TRANSFER TERM LIFE INSURANCE OR WHOLE
          LIFE THAT IS BORROWED UP TO AN IRREVOCABLE TRUST,
2.   A:   GIFT WILL PRODUCE A NET INCREASE IN FAMILY WEALTH BY
          SAVING INCOME OR TRANSFER TAXES,
     B:   PARTICULAR BENEFICIARIES NEED THE HELP,
     C:   CLIENT DESIRES TO SHIELD ASSETS FROM FUTURE BUSINESS
          RISK,
     D:   DESIRES TO BE RELIEVED OF ASSET MANAGEMENT
          RESPONSIBILITIES,
     E:   DESIRES TO AVOID PROBATE ON PARTICULAR ASSETS, OR
     F:   DESIRES TO PERSONALLY EXPERIENCE THE GRATITUDE OF BENEFICIARIES, AND
3.   GIFTS ARE UNLIKELY TO CAUSE FAMILY DISHARMONY OR THE
     CLIENT IS UNCONCERNED, THEN
          CLIENT SHOULD EXPLORE PERMANENT INTERVIVOS GIFTS
          (BACK TO QUESTION 2 . . . )
**Y


3)   WILL GIFTS PRODUCE A NET INCREASE IN FAMILY WEALTH BY
     SAVING INCOME AND/OR TRANSFER TAXES?
**Y


4)   ARE GIFTS LIKELY TO CAUSE FAMILY DISHARMONY, AND DOES
     CLIENT WISH TO AVOID THIS?
**N

I RECOMMEND THAT THE CLIENT EXPLORE PERMANENT INTERVIVOS GIFTS.
(THE SYSTEM NOW INVESTIGATES GIFTS IN DETAIL.)
```

Figure 1-5

*Partial sample user
session with BATTLE*

*Explanatory notes on this example appear in this italic type face.
The user's responses appear in **bold type face**.*

```
(please enter the desired command-level alternative or "?" for help)?
valid control level commands are

af/t - add friendly/target units
ca   - compel allocation of friendly units to targets
cf/t - change unit name of a friendly/target
fc   - free compelled friendly to target allocations
pa   - prevent allocation of friendly units to targets
fp   - free (reallow) friendly-target allocations
mf/t - modify position or type or value of friendly/target
pf/t - print the list of friendly/target units
qs   - question me on some units
qw/t - question a weapon/target with a preselected list
rf/t - remove friendly/target units from consideration
vl   - volunteering information on weapon-target pairs
vw/t - volunteer information on weapon/target
wt   - devise the weapon target allocation plans
te   - terminate program execution
?    - print out this help message
??   - print out system development commands
```

Add two friendly units to the scenario, fr-1 and fr-2.

(please enter the desired command level alternative -----) **af**

(please enter the new unit name or t) **fr-1**
(please enter the friendly fighting capacity) **300**
(please enter a valid friendly unit type) **?**

```
(valid entries include:)
art105--mm-105-artillery-unit(1)
art155--mm-155-artillery-unit(2)
art8in--inch-8-artillery-unit(3)
mrt50--mm-60-mortar(4)
mrt81--mm-81-mortar(5)
ngf--naval-battery-fire(6)
(t--terminate)
```

(please enter a valid friendly unit type) **art105**
(please enter the unit x position) **450**
(please enter the unit y position) **735**

(please enter the next unit name or t) **fr-2**
(please enter the friendly fighting capacity) **465**
(please enter a valid friendly unit type) **art155**
(please enter the unit x position) **530**
(please enter the unit y position) **240**

(please enter the next unit name or t) **t**

Figure 1-5

(continued)

Add two targets to the battlefield, tr-1 and tr-2.

```
(please enter the desired command level alternative -----) at

(please enter the new unit name or t) tr-1
(please enter the potential target value) 1000
(please enter a valid first target component type or t) ?

(valid entries include:)
art122--mm-122-artillery-unit(1)
art130--mm-130-artillery-unit(2)
art152--mm-152-artillery-unit(3)
fxd--fixed-target(4)
mrl140--mm-140-rocket-unit(5)
(t--terminate)

(please enter a valid first target component type of t) art122
(please enter the percent or art122) 100
(please enter the unit x position) 500
(please enter the unit y position) 350
```

Try to add the same unit twice.

```
(please enter the next unit name or t) tr-1
(** ? duplicate declaration ? **)

(please enter the next unit name or t) tr-2
(please enter the potential target value) 850
(please enter a valid first target component type or t) art122
(please enter the percent of art122) 50
(please enter a valid next target component type or t) art152
(please enter the percent of art152) 25
(please enter a valid next target component type or t) t
(please enter the unit x position) 395
(please enter the unit y position) 400

(please enter the next unit name or t) t
```

Now request two allocation plans for the weapons.

```
(please enter the desired command level alternative -----) wt
(please enter the number of plans desired) 2

(weapon to target allocations:)
-----------------------
(total allocation value: 701,567604)
(fr-2 attacks tr-1: effect: 0.552817 value: 552.817604)
(fr-1 attacks tr-2: effect: 0.175 value: 148.75)
                            .
                            .
                            .
```

Source: Slagle, J.R., M. W. Gaynor, and H. Hamburger. *Decision Support System for Fire Support Command and Control.* NRL Report 8769, Navy Center for Applied Research in Artificial Intelligence, Naval Research Laboratory, Washington, D.C. (December 30, 1983).

Advantages and Limitations of Expert Systems

Expert systems offer new ways to encode and employ knowledge to solve problems [1]. They are improved approaches to formalizing and handling knowledge previously thought unsuited for formal organization. Expert system applications have shown that programs can operate at or near the level of human experts. This is particularly advantageous in cases where one needs expert advice, but is unable to get a human expert due to high costs, unavailability of human experts, or time constraints. An expert system can be used to support and verify a human expert's opinion, and it can be used in situations in which an individual may become easily flustered due to time and pressure constraints.

As there are advantages of using expert systems, there are also limitations. First, the knowledge acquisition process (i.e., the learning process) is a major limitation of expert systems. Although the computer programs are fairly adept at making analyses, most cannot learn from experience. Second, there is a potential problem in the manner in which generality and specificity are simultaneously being achieved [2,14]. This leads to the difficulty of combinatorial explosion of search spaces, which is presently being handled by enabling the solver to operate within a narrow, specified context. Third, there is a difficulty in debugging programs containing large amounts of knowledge. Fourth, the expert system should be able to automate the input from various experts and integrate it, instead of having one expert acting as the sole source of knowledge. Fifth, because this field is relatively new, there is a shortage of **knowledge engineers** who are responsible for acquiring, representing, and programming expert knowledge.

Research Issues in Expert Systems

Since artificial intelligence is a newly evolving field, several areas of research are needed to improve artificial intelligence techniques. One major area of needed research pertains to knowledge acquisition/extraction. More research is warranted in developing new approaches to acquire knowledge from the domain expert(s). Having efficient and effective knowledge acquisition techniques is essential in structuring the problem domain. Efforts are underway to improve knowledge acquisition. Such efforts are:

1. developing smart editors that assist in modifying and entering rules,

2. developing an intelligent interface that can interview the expert and formulate rules, and

3. developing a learning system to induce rules from examples.

Part of this problem of inventing better knowledge acquisition methods is the shortage of artificial intelligence talent. The existence of only a nominal number of qualified knowledge engineers has crippled artificial intelligence development. This trend is somewhat reversing as more universities are offering artificial intelligence courses and curricula.

Another major area in which research is needed pertains to better understanding of analogical reasoning and learning. Expert systems are probes for analogy and tend to dampen out inference bias. Through better understanding of how humans reason and learn, this will facilitate improved techniques for development of expert systems. Research is also needed in developing expert systems that can learn from previous experiences. An important aspect is the ability for expert systems to learn so that mistakes in advice may not be repeated. This vital ingredient can not be fully encaptured in expert systems until the human learning process is better understood.

A methodology of validation needs to be developed for expert systems. A need exists for a "standard" methodology for validating expert systems, such as what has been accomplished in software engineering [25]. By having a standard, structured validation methodology, false expectations about expert system performances should be greatly lessened.

Ancillary research issues pertaining to expert system development include these:

- Improving explanation capabilities.
- Having better expert system architectures and inference procedures.
- Incorporating the ability for expert systems to make assumptions and expectations.
- Improving methods of handling uncertain, incomplete, and inconsistent information.
- Developing better user interfaces.
- Creating parallel processing approaches.

If these research issues are addressed and resolved, then expert systems will become more powerful and useful tools for many applications.

References

1. Duda, R. O., and Shortliffe, E. H., 1983. "Expert Systems Research." *Science,* 220, April 15.
2. Michie, D., 1979. *Expert Systems in the MicroElectronic Age*. Edinburgh: Edinburgh University Press.
3. Barr, A., and Feigenbaum E. A., 1981. *The Handbook of Artificial Intelligence*. Vol. 1. Los Altos, CA: HeurisTech Press.
4. Michie, D., 1980. *Knowledge-Based Systems*. University of Illinois at Urbana-Champaign, Report 80–1001.
5. Gevarter, W. B., 1982. *An Overview of Expert Systems*. National Aeronautics and Space Administration.
6. Stefik, M., Aikins, J., Balzer, R., Benoit, J., Birnbaum, L., Hayes-Roth, F., and Sacerdoti, E., 1983. "The Architecture of Expert Systems." In *Building Expert Systems*. Reading, MA: Addison-Wesley.
7. Winston, P. H., and Brown, R. H., 1979. *Artificial Intelligence: An MIT Perspective*. Vol. 1. Cambridge, MA: MIT Press.
8. Duda, R. O., and Gaschnig, J. G., 1981. "Knowledge-Based Expert Systems Come of Age." *BYTE*, September.
9. Nau, D. S., 1983. "Expert Computer Systems." *IEEE Computer*, February.
10. Software A & E, 1983. *Knowledge Engineering System: Knowledge Base Author's Reference Manual*. Arlington, VA: Software Architecture & Engineering, Inc.
11. Reggia, J. A., and Perricone, B. T., 1982. *KMS Manual*. College Park: University of Maryland.
12. Hayes-Roth, F., Klahr, P., and Mostow, D. J., 1980. *Knowledge Acquisition, Knowledge Programming, and Knowledge Refinement*. Rand Report R–2540–NSF. Santa Monica, CA: Rand Corporation.

13. Buchanan, B. G., and Shortliffe, E. H., 1984. *Rule-Based Expert Programs: The MYCIN Experiments of the Stanford Heuristic Programming Project.* Reading, MA: Addison-Wesley.

14. Michie, D., *op cit.* Also see Dreyfus, H. L., 1972. *What Computers Can't Do: A Critique of Artificial Reason.* New York: Harper & Row.

15. Sewell, H. B. (in press). *Analogical Reasoning Theory.* Washington, DC: George Washington University.

16. Gevarter, W. B., 1983. *Expert Systems: Limited but Powerful. Spectrum*, August.

17. Waterman, D. A., 1986. *A Guide to Expert Systems.* Reading, MA: Addison-Wesley.

18. Winston, P. H., and Prendergast, K. A., 1984. *The AI Business: Commercial Uses of Artificial Intelligence.* Cambridge, MA: MIT Press.

19. Weiss, S. M., and Kulikowski, C. A., 1984. *A Practical Guide to Designing Expert Systems.* Totowa, NJ: Rowman & Allanheld.

20. Brown, J. S., Burton, R. R., and DeKleer, J., 1982. "Pedagogical, Natural Language, and Knowledge Engineering Techniques in SOPHIE I, II, and III." *Intelligent Tutoring Systems.* eds. D. Sleeman and J. S. Brown. New York: Academic Press.

21. Michaelsen, R., and Michie, D., 1983. "Expert Systems in Business." *Datamation*, November.

22. Slagle, J. R., and Hamburger, H., 1985. "BATTLE: An Expert System for a Resource Allocation Problem." *Communications of the ACM*, 28, No. 9. New York: Association for Computing Machinery.

23. DeSalvo, D. A., Glamm, A. E., and Liebowitz, J., 1987. "Structured Design of an Expert System Prototype at the National Archives." In *Expert Systems in Business*, ed. B. Silverman. Reading, MA: Addison Wesley.

24. Tyner, J., 1987. "Expert System Program Seeks to Put Wisdom into Computer." *The Sun*, March 29, pp. 1C, 4C.

2 Problem Selection

In developing an expert system, the first major phase deals with problem selection. *Problem selection* refers to the identification of a problem domain and suitable task for expert system development. A *problem domain* is a particular functional area in which an expert system would be useful, such as medical diagnosis. A *task* is a specific application within the domain, such as diagnosing bacterial infections in the blood.

Problem selection is an "analysis" activity. In some ways it is similar to deciding upon the construction of a management information system. With a management information system one prepares an information analysis that outlines the present system, i.e., the problem domain. The information analysis helps the designer to understand better the inputs, processes, interactions, and outputs of the present system and to see how the present system can be improved. With expert systems, problem selection also should involve an information analysis to understand the domain and its limitations.

In addition to an information analysis, feasibility studies are usually prepared when developing a management information system. The feasibility studies indicate the economic, technical, and operational feasibilities in developing a management information system. With expert system development, feasibility studies should also be performed to determine the costs and benefits of designing and implementing an expert system.

Problem selection is the first step in the knowledge engineering process. **Knowledge engineering** is the process of building, testing, and evaluating an expert system. The individual who is responsible for the problem selection, knowledge acquisition, representation, programming, and refinement phases of developing an expert system is the *knowledge engineer.*

There are several reasons why an expert system might be helpful for a given task. First, one might need an expert who is unavailable. If an individual has a medical problem whose symptoms can be diagnosed by only a few experts, then an expert system that was developed to analyze the ailment might be helpful, particularly if the experts are unavailable. Second, an expert system might be useful for verifying one's opinion. It could be used as a "second check." Third, an expert system would be helpful under time and pressure constraints. In battle management, for example, a human may not be able to think clearly under artillery attack. An expert system, in this case, might be helpful to provide an allocation of weapons to targets. An expert system as a pilot's associate would also be advantageous to help the pilot make decisions under enemy attack. Fourth, an expert system can "document" knowledge. Knowledge can be preserved, so that an individual's forty years of experience and acquired knowledge with a company, for example, would not be "lost." The company's institutional memory would be enhanced and further developed.

Task Characteristics

Several characteristics determine a task best suited for an expert system application:

- The task is well-bounded to prevent combinatorial explosions.
- The task involves mainly symbolic processing (the processing of lists and symbols), as distinct from numerical processing.
- The task takes from a few hours to a few weeks to solve.
- The task is performed frequently (i.e., it is not a once-in-a-lifetime activity).
- There is a significant difference between the best and worst performers of the task:
- Test data is easily available.
- The solution to the task has a general consensus.
- There exists at least one expert acknowledged as such by his/her peers.
- The expert is willing to participate in the expert system development and devote the necessary time to build the expert system.
- The expert is articulate and can be understood by the knowledge engineer.

Each of these criteria will be discussed in turn.

Well-Bounded Task

The task selected for the expert system application should be well bounded to avoid combinatorial explosion. The task should encompass a narrowly specified amount of knowledge, where the knowledge comprises facts, relevant to the task and domain, and rules of thumb acquired by the expert's years of professional experience and wisdom. If the task is too broad in scope, such as to determine what to do in case of a nuclear war, then the search space will be so large that combinatorial explosion of alternatives could result. A limitation of expert systems, to date, is that expert systems' performances degrade fairly rapidly when processing knowledge outside the narrowly defined task. Part of this problem is due to the lack of learning within the expert system and the inability of the expert system to make assumptions. A practical upper limit of the solution search space for exhaustive search is 10! [1]. If 25 milliseconds are required to consider a solution, then 10! solutions can be considered sequentially during a full 24-hour day [1].

Symbolic Processing

Expert systems are most useful in tasks involving symbolic processing, instead of numerical processing. *Symbolic processing* refers to the execution of symbols (strings of characters) and symbol structures (data structures). Numerical processing can be performed by conventional high-level languages, like FORTRAN, COBOL, or BASIC. With **list-processing** languages like LISP and **logic-programming** languages like PROLOG, symbolic processing can be easily performed, which enhances the development of expert systems. For tasks involving a significant amount of numerical computation, an expert system probably would not be necessary since the calculations could be better performed through a conventional programming language. There is a recent trend in expert systems, however, in which expert systems are being developed for solving a combination of symbolic and numerical processing problems.

▌ Few Hours to a Few Weeks to Solve

If a task takes longer than a few weeks to solve, then an expert system, with today's technology, may not be helpful in solving the problem. If a solution takes more than a few weeks to solve, then the risk of combinatorial explosion would be heightened. However, there are cases, as will be shown later in the chapter, where an expert system could be useful for problems that might otherwise take one to three months to solve. The majority of the tasks used for expert systems, though, fall within the few-hours-to-few-weeks guideline. Some people [2] suggest even more stringent requirements in which expert systems should perform tasks that might otherwise take a few minutes to a few hours to solve.

▌ Task Is Performed Frequently

Frequently occurring tasks are usually selected for expert system applications. Diagnosing bacterial infections, configuring computers, tutoring in electronics, and determining telephone cable maintenance problems are examples of recurring tasks where expert systems have been successfully applied and used. Infrequently needed tasks, such as what to do in case a hurricane hits Washington, D.C., are not very practical applications for an expert system since the likelihood of occurrence is slim. The usefulness of an expert system is maximized when the expert system is used to solve a task repeatedly.

▌ Significant Difference Between the Best and Worst Performers

A task is more suitable for an expert system when there is a large discrepancy between the best and worst performers of the task [3]. The larger the margin of error between the expert and the novice in performing a task, the greater the likelihood for using that task for an expert system application. If there is a great variation between the expert and the novice, then an expert system could encapture the expert's knowledge and experience to help the novice. If there is little difference between the outcome of a task solved by an expert and that solved by a novice, then an expert system would not be as useful as if there were great disparity.

▌ Test Data Is Available

Having test data readily available for selecting a task is not a necessary criterion for expert system development. However, it is very helpful for validation and testing purposes of the expert system. With test data available, backcasting can be more effortlessly performed, where expert system cases are compared with documented, historical cases to test the expert system's quality of advice. With plenty of test cases to choose from, backcasting would be more easily accomplished and a variety of test cases would be obtained more easily.

General Consensus

A task should be selected for an expert system application when there is general agreement that a task can be solved. If the experts in a particular task do not agree on a solution, even though their approaches to determining the solution may differ, then it would be best not to develop an expert system for that task. For example, an expert system should not be developed to determine how to solve the nation's macroeconomic policy. Besides being not well-bounded, there is not a general consensus on how to determine the best macroeconomic policy. There are different views on solving the task. The Keynesians believe that the interest rate is the central factor; the Monetarists believe that the money supply is the primary component; and the Reaganomists believe in other central economic criteria. Building an expert system for determining the macroeconomic policy would be senseless since there is not general harmony on what the solution should be. Thus, pick a task where there is a general consensus of opinion on the solution to that task.

Expert Exists, Is Willing to Participate, and Is Articulate

For a task to be suitable for an expert system application, there should be at least one expert, acknowledged as such by his/her peers. Preferably, pick a task that has more than one expert in that specific area because another expert may be needed due to the first expert's unavailability, unwillingness, or possible illness. Also, it is helpful to have other domain experts for consultation and validation and evaluation of the expert system. It is difficult to say when someone is an expert. For some tasks it may take up to 20 years of professional experience and knowledge to become an expert; whereas, in other tasks, the task might be so specific and unique that someone with a few months of experience may be called an expert. The domain expert is an individual, acknowledged by peers as being an expert, who supplies the main source of knowledge in a task to the knowledge engineer. The expert generally has a keen acumen and an unusual talent for getting to the heart of the problem and solving it. He/she typically has built up a number of years of professional experience in performing the task, and has developed rules of thumb from experiential learning over the years in solving the task.

For an appropriate task for expert system development, the expert must be willing to participate and devote time out of a busy schedule to assist in the knowledge engineering process. Waterman [4] states that the expert must be nearby and able to devote up to three quarters of his/her time to the expert system effort during the first six months and up to half of his/her time thereafter. For the development of COMPASS [5], an expert system for determining telephone-switching-equipment problems, the knowledge engineering team had been meeting with the domain expert for one week per month from May 1984 to December 1986. In addition to devoting time to assist in the expert system building process, the expert must also be articulate for the knowledge engineer to understand the task at hand.

With these criteria kept in mind, the selection of an appropriate task for building an expert system will be greatly facilitated. The next few paragraphs present a case study whose focus, at this point, is on the problem-selection stage of expert system development.

Case Study: READ Introduced

An expert system prototype, called READ (Requirements Engineering Automated Development), developed by Liebowitz [6], will be described in this and forthcoming chapters. For this chapter READ will be discussed in terms of its problem situation and problem-selection stage.

Problem Situation: Description

READ is an expert system prototype that was developed for determining software functional requirements of command management activities for NASA-supported satellites. It would generate up to three levels of functional requirements to define what the system is supposed to do. These requirements, along with the operational and performance requirements, would be used to construct the software modules for a satellite's command management system. The Command Management System (CMS) at NASA Goddard Space Flight Center is responsible for sending command and control data from the user (scientists) to the satellite. It is part of the NASA Data System, which entails the downlink of science and engineering data from NASA near-earth satellites through Goddard operations to the user, and the uplink of commands from the user to the satellite.

The present way of developing the functional requirements for a new mission's CMS software is through a series of meetings, interviews, questionnaires, and documents. Usually a team of contractor personnel with varying years of professional experience is assembled to determine the functional requirements for a new mission's CMS software. Typically, this team will meet with NASA personnel, contractors, satellite project team members, and experimenters (scientists) to synthesize the functional requirements for the CMS. It can take from one to three years of meetings, once or twice a week, to ascertain a final list of functional requirements. From these requirements the necessary software can be designed to accomplish the CMS objectives.

The present technique of gathering functional requirements has various limitations:

- The present method of numerous meetings with all the parties involved is very time-consuming in ascertaining the functional requirements for CMS operation. In fact, by having these meetings and manually recording the results, it has taken one to three years for determining the final functional requirements. A "first cut" of software functional requirements takes about one to three months to develop.

- Additionally, the team contracted to develop the functional requirements may not consist solely of individuals with many years of professional experience in this area because these persons are few in number and they may be assigned to different tasks within the company. This places a limitation on the wealth of knowledge in terms of professional experience and expertise for determining functional requirements, prolonging the time necessary to determine the CMS functional requirements.

- Another element compounding this problem situation is the external pressures of greater frequency of shuttle launches and less lead time available to develop a new mission's ground system. With less lead time available for the ground system design of a new mission, the luxury of taking up to three years to develop the functional requirements is vanishing.

- Last, a corollary to the second aforementioned system limitation is the reliance upon a handful of individuals who have the professional experience and expertise to determine the functional requirements for CMS software development. This is the major problem under the status quo. To decrease reliance on these individuals, it would be beneficial to NASA to have some automated way of capturing the professional experience of these experts before they leave.

The expert's reasoning process in determining CMS software functional requirements follows closely the five steps of analogical reasoning outlined in Silverman [7]. These steps are problem identification, knowledge acquisition, analog transfer, analog transformation, and introduction into use. In *problem identification*, the expert tries to understand the overall purpose of the satellite mission. He/she accomplishes this through the *knowledge acquisition stage* in which NASA-generated and contractor-generated documentation and discussions between NASA personnel and contractors play vital roles. The contractor expert is given a NASA-generated Functional Specifications Document, which is a "wish list" of requirements specified by satellite experimenters and NASA personnel for the new satellite. This document is prepared approximately six or seven years before satellite launch, and the requirements are generally not grouped by function. After carefully reading this document, the contractor expert develops bubble flow diagrams to group the functional specifications into logical areas (e.g., database management function). Once this is completed, the expert meets once or twice a week for one to three years with users of the new satellite (i.e., NASA satellite project team, NASA personnel, satellite experimenters, and contractors) to develop the functional requirements needed for CMS software design. These discussions are feedback sessions that serve as filters in the expert's reasoning process in developing functional requirements. The expert is trying to weed out the problem areas that relate to complicated requirements demanded by the satellite users.

Once these problem areas are identified, the *analog transfer* stage occurs, in which the expert refers to previous satellites to see how these problem areas were handled in the past. If functional requirements for these problem areas were developed for previous satellites, the same set of functional requirements could be used, or this set of requirements could be used as a base and improved upon for the new satellite (due to technological advances). After identifying past similar functional requirements, the expert uses *analog transformation* to transform the past similar requirements to fit the new satellite's mission. *Introduction into use* then occurs by documenting the functional requirements for the new satellite into the Functional Requirements Document.

A major reason for the need for a new approach for developing CMS software requirements is to enhance analogical analysis. Analogical analysis needs to be enhanced because of an inadequate knowledge base resulting from bias pollution, and because of an inadequate procedure for inference. Analogical analysis is predicated upon drawing inference. Optimizing analogical analysis entails minimizing biases in the inference. Inference bias comes primarily from the interactions between the values and views of the CMS designer [8]. Through the use of an expert system, bias is dampened out because a computer is being used to act as the inference engine. The combination of the software and hardware dampens out bias because expert systems don't have dynamic interactions of values and views. By reducing the bias pollution used in drawing inferences, the resulting knowledge base can become purer than that without the use of an expert system.

▌ Problem Selection

For the command management system activities at NASA Goddard, there is a need for a new approach to aid in the development of software requirements. By having an expert system that could capture the expert's professional experience and knowledge, the analogical value of previous experience could be fully utilized. The pertinency of the knowledge base would be purer and this would help to represent a better fit between the CMS software requirements and the satellite program requirements.

The *problem domain* for this expert system is the Command Management System at NASA Goddard Space Flight Center. The specific *task* is the development of software functional requirements for command management activities of NASA-supported satellites. This task is *well-bounded* as the focus is on functional requirements, not including performance and operational requirements, which are different. Functional requirements describe what the system is supposed to do. Performance requirements are concerned with how quickly, how many, and how often requirements should be executed. Operational requirements concentrate on what the system is supposed to "look like" to the user. If the task included performance and operational requirements as well as functional requirements, then the task would have been unmanageable and perhaps would have led to combinatorial explosion.

The task involves *symbolic processing* as compared with numerical processing. The manipulation of words and phrases (e.g., nature of the mission, safety considerations) was prevalent in the development of functional requirements. The only numerical processing involved the calculation of certainty factors for handling uncertainty in the expert system. The task of developing functional requirements is performed each time a new satellite is proposed, thus making this task *frequently* performed. Documents of previous satellite functional requirements facilitated the generation of *test cases* for backcasting and validation of the expert system. One sore point, however, was that no standardized requirements language was used from one satellite to another. This created some problems in the backcasting process, as explained in Chapter 8, as the same requirement might have been worded differently from one satellite to the next.

The task of developing a "first cut" of software functional requirements for the CMS design of a satellite took from one to three months. A final list of functional requirements took from one to three years. READ is supposed to generate a first cut of functional requirements, up to three levels. Even though the task slightly exceeded the general guideline of taking a *few hours to a few weeks* to solve, it still was a manageable task. It was a particularly good task because there was a *significant difference between the expert and novice* CMS designer. An individual who has a few years of professional experience in the CMS task environment may ask (and re-ask) four or five questions to get to the heart of a functional requirement; whereas an expert or an individual with many years of experience in the CMS environment might have to ask only one question for determining a particular functional requirement [9]. Also, the *solution to the task* had a general consensus.

In terms of the expert's availability, there were two or three *experts* in determining CMS software functional requirements. One of these experts was *willing to participate* in the construction of READ, was able to *devote the necessary time* in the knowledge engineering process, and was *very articulate*.

Based upon these problem selection criteria, an expert system approach was selected for solving the task of developing CMS software functional requirements for NASA-supported satellites.

The next chapter will describe the second step in the expert system building process, namely, knowledge acquisition.

References

1. Stefik, M., Aikins, J., Balzer, R., Benoit, J., Birnbaum, L., Hayes-Roth, F., and Sacerdoti, E., 1983. "The Architecture of Expert Systems." In *Building Expert Systems*. Reading, MA: Addison-Wesley.

2. Feigenbaum, E. A., 1982. Lecture on Expert Systems. At George Washington University, Washington, DC, October 15.

3. Harmon, P., and King, D., 1985. *Artificial Intelligence in Business: Expert Systems*. New York: John Wiley & Sons.

4. Waterman, D. A., 1986. *A Guide to Expert Systems*. Reading, MA: Addison-Wesley.

5. Prerau, D. S., Gunderson, A. S., Reinke, R. E., and Goyal, S. K., 1985. "The COMPASS Expert System: Verification, Technology Transfer, and Expansion." In *Proceedings of the Second Conference on Artificial Intelligence Applications*. Washington, DC: IEEE. December 11–13.

6. Liebowitz, J., 1985. *Determining Functional Requirements for NASA Goddard's Command Management System Software Design Using Expert Systems*. D.Sc. dissertation, George Washington University, Washington, DC.

7. Silverman, B. G., 1983. "The Use of Analogs in Systems Engineering: A Software Programming Case Study." *Engineering Administration Report*. Washington, DC: George Washington University.

8. Sewell, H. B., (in press). *Analogical Reasoning Theory*. Washington, DC: George Washington University.

9. Discussions with Computer Sciences Corporation. Silver Spring, MD. August–October 1983.

3 | Knowledge Acquisition

After selecting an appropriate problem or task for expert system development, the next major step in building an expert system deals with knowledge acquisition. Before discussing this phase of the life cycle development process, we will take a step backwards and give some advice on the resources needed to build an expert system, as well as suggest some helpful hints in constructing an expert system.

Expert System Building Hints and Resources

Building an expert system is an iterative and evolutionary process. The steps of knowledge acquisition, knowledge representation, knowledge programming, and knowledge testing and evaluation are iteratively performed throughout the development of the expert system. The knowledge base should constantly be refined, through increasing the knowledge and filtering out imperfections and biases in the knowledge base. The approach most used in developing expert systems is rapid prototyping. **Rapid prototyping** involves modeling a subset of the task where system design, coding, and testing are performed on that subset [1]. Then, through iterative refinements, the subset is modified, enhanced, and enlarged to encompass the total task. Here the complete life cycle process is performed on successive pieces of the task. The important point is that the knowledge engineer should, as soon as possible, start encoding the knowledge acquired from the expert to develop the expert system software. The knowledge engineer should encode the knowledge based on a subset of the task, and then perform knowledge testing and evaluation, with the help of the expert, on that part of the expert system. Through testing and evaluation of the expert system prototype, it might be discovered that the knowledge representation method or inference mechanism is not efficient. Here the knowledge might be better represented as frames instead of rules (this will be discussed in Chapter 4), or perhaps forward chaining should be used instead of backward chaining (this will be explained in Chapter 5). By "getting to the code" as early as possible, these issues can be addressed before the full-scale expert system is built. By doing rapid prototyping, the knowledge engineer should expect to build several iterations of the expert system, with the strong probability that there will be some "throw-away" versions of the expert system prototype. Typically, a demonstration version of the expert system prototype is developed to convince management that the approach is feasible and that the eventual full-scale expert system development should be approved. Then the expert system prototype is further developed and is tested in the "field." Eventually, after knowledge refinement, testing, and evaluation activities, the full-scale expert system is designed and implemented.

Hayes-Roth [2] has developed the following heuristic rules about knowledge bases:

- An interesting demonstration of the technology requires only 50 rules.
- A convincing demonstration of a knowledge system's power requires about 250 rules.
- A commercially practical system may require as few as 50 rules.
- An expert level of competence in a narrow area requires about 500 to 1000 rules.
- Expertise in a profession requires about 10,000 rules.
- The limit of human expertise is about 100,000 rules.

The resources and time needed to develop expert systems vary greatly. Harmon and King [3] state that for a small system of 50 to 350 rules, it may take 1/4 to 1/2 person-years to develop the expert system at a project cost of $40,000 to $60,000. Cost includes design, development, knowledge engineers, computing, and overhead. For a large expert system of 500 to 3000 rules, it may take 1 to 2 person-years and $500,000 to $1 million to develop an expert system. For a very large expert system of about 10,000 rules, it may take 3 to 5 person-years and $2 million to $5 million to develop the expert system [3]. Waterman [4] estimates the following requirements for a moderately difficult task:

- **Effort:** 6 person-years
- **Time:** 2 years
- **Staff:**

Senior knowledge engineer	0.25
Junior knowledge engineer	1.00
AI programmer	1.00
Domain expert	<u>0.75</u>
Total full-time professionals	3.00

Johnson [5] states:

> Once the team settles on an application, it must then convince management to finance its project. The cost of building a prototype is $1 million to $3 million, estimate consultants. That endowment covers computer equipment, software tools, staff time and training, and, of course, the ever present, high-dollar consultant or two. If a company is not willing to go that distance, to spend that much, the team can forget pulling together a "serious" but small demonstration prototype system, suggest industry consultants. To move from a prototype to a production system, add another year or two and another $1 million to $3 million.

Johnson's prediction of costs are inflated. With available expert system shells that facilitate construction of expert systems (as will be discussed in Chapter 6), the costs of building expert systems are greatly reduced. The cost of an expert system shell varies from simple microcomputer-based shells starting at $49 to minicomputer- and mainframe-based shells costing up to $72,000.

▋ Expert System Building Tips

The following are some helpful expert system construction hints, per the works of Hayes-Roth et al. [2], Feigenbaum and McCorduck [6], Parsaye [7], Liebowitz [8], and Johnson [5]:

TASK SUITABILITY

- Focus on a narrow specialty area that does not involve a lot of common-sense knowledge.
- Select a task that is neither too easy nor too difficult for human experts.
- Define the task very closely.
- Commitment from an articulate expert is essential.
- Expert systems could have great payoffs in mundane tasks, not necessarily heroic ones.
- Pick a task that will have a significant impact of value to the organization.

BUILDING A PROTOTYPE

- Become familiar with the problem before beginning extensive interaction with the expert.
- Clearly identify and characterize the important aspects of the problem.
- Record a detailed protocol of the expert solving at least 1 prototypical case.
- Choose a knowledge engineering tool or architecture that minimizes the representational mismatch between subproblems.
- Start building the prototype version of the expert system as soon as the first example is well understood.
- Work intensively with a core set of representative problems.
- Identify and separate the parts of the problem that have caused trouble for AI programs in the past.
- Build in mechanisms for indirect reference.
- Separate domain-specific knowledge from general problem-solving knowledge.
- Aim for simplicity in the inference engine.
- Don't worry about time and space efficiency in the beginning.
- Find or build computerized tools to assist in the rule-writing process.
- Pay attention to documentation.
- Don't wait until the informal rules are perfect before starting to build the system.
- When testing the system, consider the possibility of errors in input/output characteristics, inference rules, control strategies, and test examples.
- It is good to have redundancy in the expert system to give stability to the system (have multiple evidence).
- Have dynamic explanations, not static ones.
- Sometimes it might be better to try to get the surface-level rules as opposed to the deep-level knowledge.
- From the beginning, the knowledge engineer must count on throwing efforts away.
- There is a perfect task for every expert system shell or tool, but there is *not* a perfect shell or tool for every task.

EXTEND PROTOTYPE

- Build a friendly interface to the system soon after the first prototype is finished.
- Provide a "gripe" facility so users can record their complaints about the system without the knowledge engineer being there.
- Keep a library of cases presented to the system.
- It would be wonderful to have multi-layered explanations—ones for the expert, ones for the apprentice, and ones for the end-user.
- If none of the tools you normally use works, build a new one.
- Dealing with anything but facts implies uncertainty.
- The expert system must have very easy ways of allowing the knowledge to be modified so that new information can be added and out-of-date information deleted.

EXPERT

- Give the expert something useful in the line of building a large system.
- Expert will modify rules and values until he/she finds the right answer.
- Insulate the expert, as well as the user, from technical problems.
- Be careful about feeling expert.

EVALUATING THE SYSTEM

- Ask early about how the expert would evaluate the performance of the system (i.e., criteria, error rate).
- The user interface is crucial to the ultimate acceptance of the system.
- Use blind verification studies for testing and validation.

With these tips from the sources mentioned above, the job of the knowledge engineer will be made much easier.

Knowledge Acquisition

After the problem domain and suitable task are selected, the next step for building an expert system is knowledge acquisition. This is the process whereby the knowledge engineer extracts the facts and heuristics associated with the task and its environment from the expert. It is an ongoing procedure during the expert system's development to continually refine and purify the knowledge base. It is very important to have a complete, accurate, and consistent knowledge base. If the inference engine works efficiently but the knowledge base is "incomplete," then the expert system will not be effective.

Knowledge acquisition is perhaps the biggest bottleneck in expert system development. There are many reasons for this. First, biases are unintentionally imparted during the knowledge acquisition process by both the expert and the knowledge engineer. These biases inhibit the transfer of knowledge between the knowledge engineer and the expert.

The first such bias deals with intuitive statistical analysis [9]. Humans are not good as intuitive statisticians. For example, "humans do not intuitively understand the effect of sample size or variance and therefore draw unwarranted conclusions from small samples or a small number of occurrences" [9]. Also, humans have a tendency to identify causality with joint occurrence and assign cause where none exists. Studies have also shown that humans show little or no regard for considerations of predictability.

Besides having poor intuitive statistical analysis abilities, humans are influenced by a judgmental heuristic called "availability." Under "availability," biases result due to the retrievability of instances [10]. This means that when the size of a class is judged by the availability of its instances, a class whose instances are easily retrieved will appear more numerous than a class of equal frequency whose instances are less retrievable. Biases of imaginability and illusory correlation also play important roles in affecting an expert's judgement. Depending upon how vivid an expert's imagination, this will affect the evaluation of probabilities in real-life situations. Illusory correlation pertains to the associative connections between events. Humans often overestimate the frequency of co-occurrence of natural associates, such as suspiciousness and peculiar eyes [10].

Another bias affecting an expert's judgment deals with anchoring and adjustment [9,10]. Humans have a tendency to make judgments by establishing an anchor point and then making adjustments from this point [9]. This leads to biases in the evaluation of conjunctive and disjunctive events. The chain-like structure of conjunctions leads to over-estimation, and the funnel-like structure of disjunctions leads to underestimation [10].

Other biases affect an expert's, as well as the knowledge engineer's, reasoning process. One such bias deals with "recency." This relates to humans being influenced more by recent events than by past events [9]. Another bias is concreteness, in which humans tend to use the available information only in the form in which it is displayed. Humans tend not to search for data or transform or manipulate data that is presented [9].

Silverman [11] points out other aspects that lead to human error and inadequate models. These elements are related to analogical reasoning:

- Suboptimal level of schema abstraction,
- Sheer size/complexity of the schema,
- Inappropriate cues,
- Forgetting heuristics,
- Too little/too much information,
- False recoveries,
- Inappropriateness of certain verification processes.

These biases plague the knowledge acquisition process, causing imperfect knowledge to be transferred from the expert to the knowledge engineer. With the iterative process of knowledge refinement, most of these biases are filtered out of the knowledge base. However, until this is done, the expert system will produce a variety of unexpected results due to the following behavioral deficiencies [12]:

1. The expert neglected to express rules to cover all of the special cases that arise,

2. The expert's rules did not produce correct conclusions because erroneous assumptions were made,

3. Although the knowledge engineer's implementation decisions were consistent with ambiguities in the original specifications, they generated undesirable behaviors,

4. The knowledge engineer overlooked or incorrectly interpreted and implemented some of the expert's advice.

Another problem that the knowledge engineer experiences during knowledge acquisition is the lack of knowledge about the problem domain and task environment. It is vital that the knowledge engineer should become familiar with the problem domain and specific task *before* starting the knowledge acquisition sessions with the expert. The knowledge engineer should speak with appropriate individuals performing the task at hand, should read documentation and manuals about the task and problem domain, should observe those doing the task, and should study the flow of information and data that results before, during, and after the task. Without the knowledge engineer being well-versed in the language, acronyms, and general system components, he/she will not be able adequately to understand the expert's explanations and will not be able to ask the right kinds of questions to extract the expert's knowledge. It is very helpful during the knowledge acquisition process if the knowledge engineer is allowed to record the sessions with the expert.

Another major problem with knowledge acquisition concerns the ability of the knowledge engineer to "probe" the expert's mind to obtain the pertinent facts and rules of thumb from the expert. The usual process for extracting knowledge is through interviews, where scenarios are proposed by the knowledge engineer, and the expert elaborates on the actions from the scenarios and possible side-effects (as will be discussed later in the chapter). What the expert takes for granted or as common sense, the knowledge engineer probably does not. This causes difficulty in extracting these "common sense" rules from the expert, mainly because the expert applies some of his/her rules of thumb, acquired through many years of professional experience, perhaps without awareness of doing so. This relates to short-term versus long-term memory limitations. Short-term memory refers to recalling items soon after they have been presented to an individual. Short-term memory is influenced by many biases, particularly the "recency" bias described above, and the expert may be able to recall some of these tip-of-the-tongue facts from the task that he/she is *currently* working on. It is more difficult for the expert to dig into his/her long-term memory to uncover knowledge and rules of thumb relevant to the problem domain and task. The knowledge engineer must be able to "trigger" the expert's long-term memory to discover these facts. This is a tough job to accomplish, but the facts can be uncovered by posing scenarios to the expert.

Methods for Performing Knowledge Acquisition

The first class of methods for transferring expertise deals with *manual* techniques. The manual approaches most used for knowledge acquisition are interviews and questionnaires. The knowledge engineer extracts knowledge from the expert through interviews and encodes the knowledge into the expert system. The knowledge engineer, after becoming familiar with the task and problem domain, will ask questions of the expert to uncover the underlying characteristics or attributes that influence the goal of the task. For example, if the goal of the task is to select who should be the U.S. President, the expert, who is a political analyst, might identify important attributes used in making that decision, such as previous record, age, eloquence, and appearance. The knowledge engineer usually creates scenarios and poses them to the expert to uncover the relevant facts and rules of thumb of the task, in this case, presidential selection. For example, part of the sample dialogue between the knowledge engineer (KE) and the expert for the task of presidential selection might be this:

```
KE:  When you are choosing a president, what factors do you
consider?

EXPERT:  Well, most people are concerned with age, previous
experience, influence on Capitol Hill, appearance, and
demeanor.

KE:  What do you mean by "demeanor"?

EXPERT:  Demeanor involves speaking ability, intelligence, and
stylish and calm actions.

KE:  What if a presidential candidate doesn't speak well?

EXPERT:  In my experience, if an individual doesn't speak well
then he has a slim chance of winning.

KE:  Say that a presidential candidate speaks well, is
handsome/attractive, and is very intelligent; however, he/she
has a poor influence on the Hill.  What characteristics must
the candidate then possess to win the election?
```

.
.
.

In this dialogue the knowledge engineer, through discussions with the expert, tries to identify the important attributes and their relationships for solving a task. **Attributes** are properties associated with objects that denote declarative (and sometimes procedural) knowledge. To organize these attributes so as better to manage the knowledge, an attribute hierarchy (sometimes called a "characteristic chart") should be constructed by the knowledge engineer. An **attribute hierarchy** is a structure that shows the hierarchical relationship of attributes used in constructing the knowledge base. Figure 3-1 shows part of a simple attribute hierarchy for determining whom to vote for as U.S. President. The bottom row of attributes are called *input* attributes, as these must be input by the user. The middle row of attributes are *inferred* attributes and are deduced from the values of the input attributes. Finally, the goal is determined, based upon these inferred attributes. The hierarchy helps in putting the important attributes and relationships into some framework. This aids in the knowledge representation phase of the expert system development process.

To obtain more specific information about the task, the knowledge engineer may also give questionnaires to the expert to answer. Questionnaires are very useful to help clarify the knowledge engineer's uncertainties about information acquired from the expert. They may also be useful when the expert may not have enough time during the day to meet with the knowledge engineer. By having the expert take home a questionnaire to answer at leisure, this may help clarify questions that otherwise the expert may not have had time to answer during a particular session with the knowledge engineer. It is much better, however, to interview the expert, as a questionnaire is impersonal and, therefore, does not allow synergistic interactions between the knowledge engineer and the expert.

Figure 3-1

Problem-Oriented Attribute Hierarchy for Determining Whom to Vote for as U.S. President

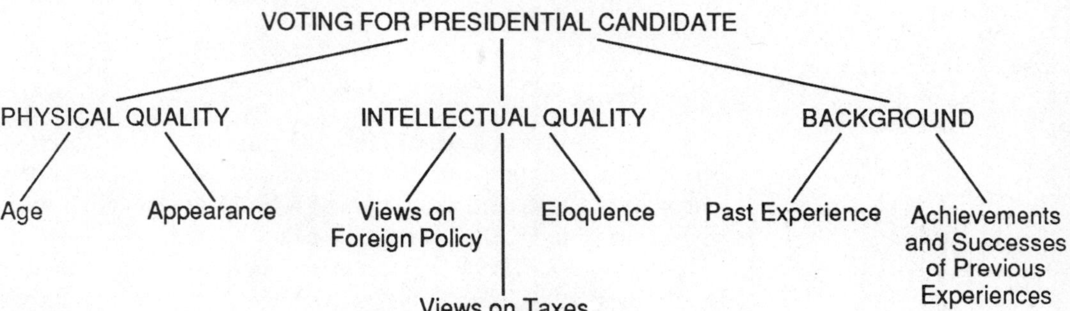

Another class of methods for acquiring knowledge for expert system development are *automated* ways for transferring expertise. In this manner knowledge acquisition can be achieved by various types of **learning**: learning by being told, learning by observation/ example, and learning by analogy. *Learning by being told* involves knowledge acquisition by interactive dialogue between the expert system and the expert. Through interactive editing, the expert system learns from the expert where the knowledge engineer is the teaching assistant [7]. Here reliance exists upon a very high-level user interface and editor. This is still very experimental, but has had some success with knowledge acquisition by interactive question asking (Marvin) and by natural language dialogue (Klaus) [7]. *Learning by observation* involves knowledge acquisition by looking at data and examples [7]. To accomplish learning by example, inductive logic is typically used. *Inductive logic* is reasoning from the particular to the general; whereas *deductive logic* involves reasoning from the general to the specific. Examples of machine learning are AM/Eurisko [13] and Aq/11 [14]. *Learning by analogy* can also be used for knowledge acquisition. An expert system might be able to reason by analogy through the following means [15]:

1.   performing an analysis of the first thing (the Base) into some abstract description (or deep structure) consisting of a problem—solution pair;

2.   performing an analysis of the second thing (the Target) into another abstract description, this time of a problem alone (the solution is as yet unknown); and

3.   performing a relevant mapping between the two descriptions that permits the solution to the target problem somehow to be determined.

The analogical process is intrinsically based on inferring. Winston [16–18], Brown [19], Sternberg [20], Gick and Holyoak [21], Rumelhart and Abrahamson [22], Carbonell [23], and Eliot [29] have been exploring the use of learning by analogy.

Other work has been done to develop automated tools for aiding in knowledge acquisition. KAS (Knowledge Acquisition System) [24], derived from PROSPECTOR [25], an expert system designed for mineral exploration, is a skeletal knowledge engineering language for rule-based representation [4]. Davis' TEIRESIAS [26] facilitates the interactive transfer of knowledge from an expert to a knowledge base. Boose's Expertise Transfer System (ETS) [30] is an automated tool that uses the rating grid technique [31] to extract knowledge from the expert. Lenat et al. [32] are trying to improve the knowledge acquisition process by building common-sense reasoning into the expert system. Quinlan's ID3/ID4 algorithms have also been developed to allow expert systems to deduce rules from data collected. Other systems are being developed to aid in the knowledge acquisition process, but these are just starting and have difficult roads ahead of them.

Case Study: READ Revisited

In Chapter 2 READ was discussed in terms of its problem-selection stage. READ is an expert system prototype designed to determine software functional requirements for command management activities of NASA Goddard-supported satellites. The knowledge acquisition stage will be described now.

Before the knowledge engineer entered into discussions with the expert, the knowledge engineer spent about two years learning the terminology, acronyms, and systems components and their functions in the NASA problem domain. NASA personnel would use "household" words, such as SMM and DE, for satellites, and words such as TELOPS and CMS for operations. Without a knowledge of these terms and what they represented, it would have been very difficult to understand what the expert was saying during the knowledge acquisition interviewing process. In some problem domains, it might take only five months to become familiar with the domain. The important factor is that the knowledge engineer should spend an adequate amount of time reading manuals and documentation and speaking to the users involved in the task before interviewing the expert for acquiring knowledge. The knowledge engineer will better understand the expert and will be able to ask appropriate and insightful questions during the interviews only when he/she has built a firm foundation on the subject dealing with the problem domain.

After building this foundation, the knowledge engineer began the interviews with the expert to formulate the attribute hierarchy. The expert was a NASA representative who had acquired over fifteen years of experience working in the command management area, and she was acknowledged as an expert by her peers. The attribute hierarchy serves as a pictorial diagram in representing the association of components, or attributes, which ultimately leads to the decision(s) or ultimate goal(s) reached by the expert system. An excerpt of the attribute hierarchy for determining CMS software functional requirements is shown in Figure 3-2. Appendix A shows the full attribute hierarchy, which depicts all the attributes and their associated level(s) in the hierarchy.

The fragment of the attribute hierarchy in Figure 3-2 depicts the ultimate goal shown at the top level—to obtain third-level CMS software functional requirements. The bottom of the hierarchy consists of attributes that determine level 1 functional requirements (which eventually lead to level 3 requirements). In this case the values of these attributes must be supplied by the end-user, and are thus called input attributes [27]. All the noncircled attributes in Figure 3-2 are input attributes. The middle level of the hierarchy depicts intermediate inferred attributes (i.e., level 1 functional requirements, circum, level

2 functional requirements) whose values are inferred from the input attributes. The goal at the top level (level 3 functional requirements) is also an inferred attribute, as its value is inferred from the intermediate inferred attributes.

Figure 3-2

Basic Structure of problem-oriented attribute hierarchy for determining CMS software functional requirements (not all attributes are shown)

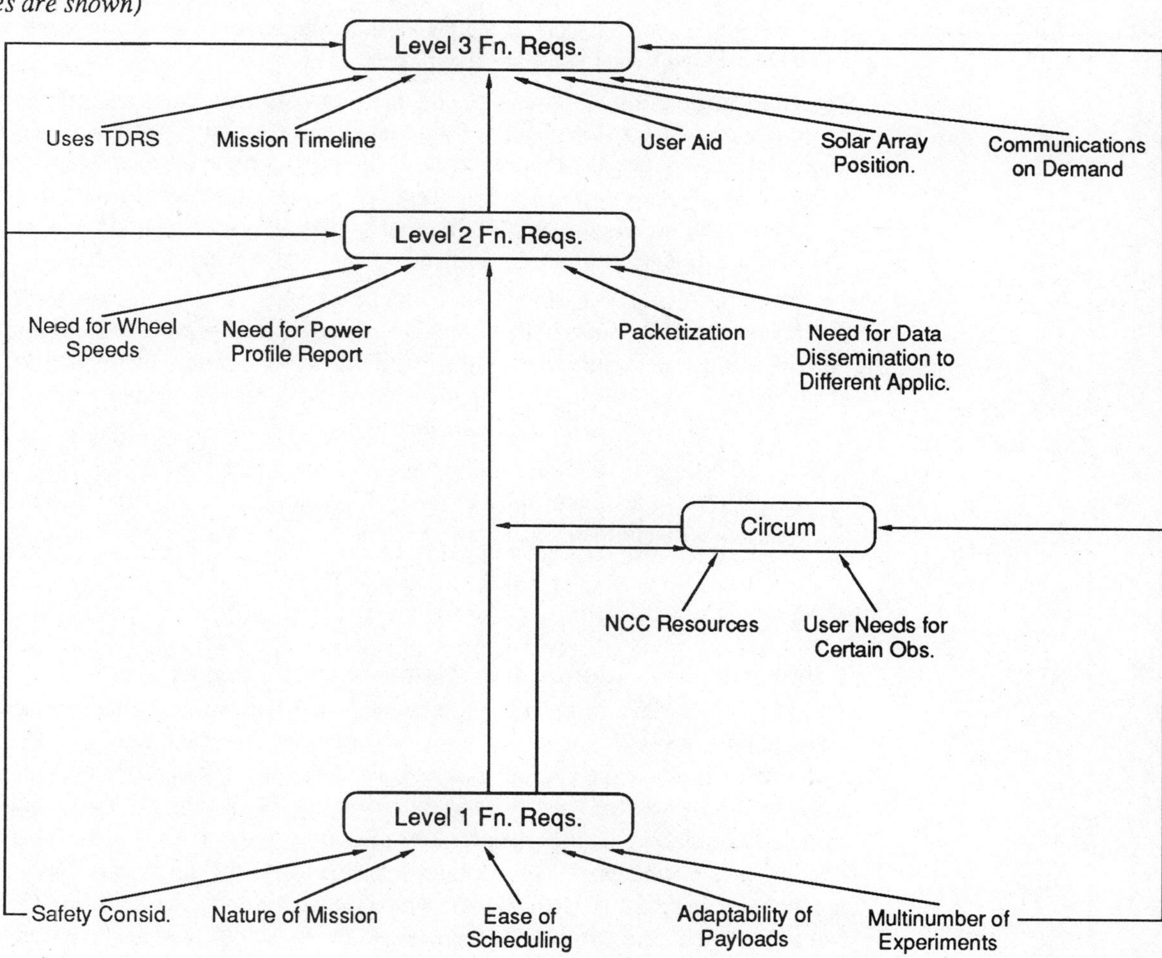

To develop the attribute hierarchy for determining CMS software functional requirements, up to three levels, the following steps were used in order:

1. Reviewed and studied NASA documents and contractor-generated reports to determine what influences CMS software functional requirements. In particular, the thrust was

on discovering the characteristics, or input attributes, that determined a satellite's CMS software functional requirements. These characteristics represent the bottom line of the attribute hierarchy. These input attributes represent questions to the user.

2.   Met with the domain expert to confirm these characteristics and to develop a complete list of characteristics, as additions and deletions were needed.

3.   Through consultations with the domain expert, it was agreed that the knowledge base, as a first cut, should be modeled after the CMS software functional requirements of the *most comprehensive* satellite to date. The reason for this thinking was that the most complex satellite would have the most exhaustive list of software functional requirements. Thus it would be easier to delete requirements for a less sophisticated satellite than it would be to add many requirements. Using this logic, Space Telescope (ST), scheduled for launch in 1989, was used as the model for developing CMS software functional requirements. Since ST represented one of the three future classes of satellite missions, using ST seemed to be a reasonable approach.

4.   After reading through numerous ST requirements documents and talking with the domain expert, the level one CMS software functional requirements were developed. This level represented the next tier above the bottom level in the attribute hierarchy. After lengthy discussions with the expert, the bottom level attributes were linked to the level one software functional requirements. In other words, the determination was made as to "which bottom level attributes influenced which level one requirements."

5.   Next, the level two CMS software functional requirements were developed via ST documents and discussions with the domain expert. Then the expert related what bottom-level characteristics (attributes) influence the level two requirements and what other attributes influence how to get from level one to the level two requirements.

6.   Last, the level three CMS software functional requirements were determined through reading ST documents and discussing the information with the expert. Then the expert related the bottom level attributes to the level three requirements and also determined other attributes that influence how to get from the level two to the level three requirements.

❙ Transcript of a Sample Discussion with the Expert

To understand further the knowledge acquisition stage of extracting the knowledge from the domain expert for knowledge base development, a partial transcript of a sample discussion with the expert is included below. This transcript describes the interactions between the knowledge engineer and the expert for CMS software functional requirements determination. This partial transcript discusses the interrelationships between the bottom-level attributes in the attribute hierarchy and the level two CMS software functional requirements. This transcript also shows the expert explaining how the level two requirements are derived. After showing the transcript, various observations from interacting with the expert will be listed.

```
KE:  I've gone to the next step in looking at the level two
functional requirements.  At this point I'm trying to relate
the characteristics (bottom-level attributes) that pertain to
the second-level requirements.  For example, if there is a
```

multinumber of experiments, then maybe you need some way to accept schedule requests.

EXPERT: These are the functions (bottom-level attributes) from a user's viewpoint.

KE: Yes.

EXPERT: If I were a PI (principal investigator), these are the functions that I could probably very clearly state. These here (level-two requirements) are functions of the way Goddard does business or the way you actually have to operate. I'm with you!

KE: Does that seem to be a fair way of doing this?

EXPERT: Yes--because a PI will typically know that these (bottom-level attributes) are things that he wants done, but he is not certain how he is going to get them done. And by getting these things (bottom-level attributes) resolved, they you could say, "Yes, I need mission scheduling and planning" (first-level functional requirement). Then up here you're telling him--well, I've told you I need mission scheduling and planning and these are the elements that need mission scheduling and planning--which of these elements I need. Okay. I got ya!

KE: So, I guess the idea is to develop some attribute hierarchy of the different characteristics that apply to each functional area to get to the second-level requirements. For example, if you take each requirement at this level (second level), then how do you arrive at each requirement? Now you may not pay attention to these characteristics (bottom-level requirements), but through your own knowledge, how would you derive each requirement?

EXPERT: Let's start with command loading. This is derived because we have a requirement to make the system user-friendly. Once a user says that he want to do command loading, then this is just a need to translate user-friendliness. Here we are talking about real-time user response. There is probably a further breakdown of this box into whether or not the user is a man or computer. If the user is a computer, then maybe this translation line that he has, doesn't have to take place. This translation line is really at the user's site and therefore the user has already made that translation. Are you with me?

KE: Yes. If the user is a man, though, . . .

EXPERT: If the user is a man, then, yes, there is really a two-way arrow when we functionally talk about getting command,

```
loading data in, and then getting that information back to him
again, telling him what we did.  Now we can tell him it's
binary and what we did, but that's not very usable to anyone.
So on the back link, you typically need this (information
feedback) coming back to the user, but you may not need it
forward coming to the user, depending on what's on the user
end.  So that is where you get involved with real-time user
response.

KE:  I see.

EXPERT:  Looking here at building the stored command processor
loads, you back out and you get to building the loads, and then
you back into command loading.  But you say why is it that you
want to build loads?  The key letter is the "s" on loads.  This
means that we have a multinumber of experimenters who may or
may not be physically located together.  So this really
reflects the need for coordination.

KE:  Would any of these other characteristics (bottom-level
attributes) apply? . . .
```

Observations from Interacting with the Domain Expert

The following is a list of observations made from the interactions between the knowledge engineer and the domain expert. This list, though some items are common sense, should be helpful to future knowledge engineers involved in knowledge acquisition and knowledge base development.

1. The knowledge engineer should make sure the expert can commit a satisfactory amount of time to work with him/her and within the time frame allotted for knowledge base development. Beware of experts who travel frequently and usually get reassigned to different tasks within their organizations.

2. The knowledge engineer should find out how much time can be spent with the expert for each session and prepare the contents of each session in advance.

3. The knowledge engineer should be patient. He/she must work around the schedule of the expert even if it means meeting every ten to fourteen days. A schedule should be set up in advance over a six-months to on- year period to establish meeting dates and times with the expert.

4. The expert may tend to go off on tangents, but the knowledge engineer should be aware of this and diplomatically bring him/her back on track.

5. The knowledge engineer should make sure that he/she has substantive work to accomplish and *results to show* at each meeting with the expert. Otherwise, the expert can't measure the progress of the knowledge engineer and the expert may feel that the knowledge engineer is wasting his/her time. That is why it is important for the knowledge engineer to start coding as soon as possible, so the expert can try the expert system to identify strengths and weaknesses for knowledge refinement.

6.	The expert must feel the project is valuable; otherwise, pick someone else.

7.	The knowledge engineer should have an orderly approach to extract the expert's knowledge, like using scenarios or stepwise additions/improvements to an attribute hierarchy. Otherwise, the expert may ramble and the knowledge engineer may not get the needed information.

8.	The knowledge engineer should use a tape recorder, if the expert allows, and also should take notes during each session.

9.	The knowledge engineer should make sure the expert's boss feels the project is worthy. Otherwise, the boss may tell the expert, during the knowledge base development, not to deal with the knowledge engineer. The knowledge engineer could be left "high and dry." To avoid this potential problem, the knowledge engineer should have the financial and moral commitment and support of top management. Also, it might be helpful to have a backup expert at hand in case something happens to the main expert.

For other general observations during the knowledge acquisition stage, the reader should consult Hayes-Roth et al. [2], Davis [28], and Reboh [24].

It turned out that the knowledge acquisition stage (not including the two years for gaining background on the problem domain) for developing READ took about 33.4% of READ's development time. The main activity during the knowledge acquisition stage was developing the attribute hierarchy.

Knowledge acquisition activities of expert systems, other than READ, have taken considerable amounts of time. The knowledge engineering team that developed COMPASS, an expert system by GTE Labs for finding faults in telephone exchanges, met with the domain expert one week a month for 18 months. An expert system prototype developed to act as an "archivist's assistant," as detailed in Appendix C, took 180 hours of the expert archivist's time spent in knowledge acquisition over a three-month development period.

The next chapter discusses knowledge representation, which follows knowledge acquisition in the expert system development life cycle.

References

1.	Chien, Y. T., and Liebowitz, J., 1986. "An Investigation of Expert Systems Usage for Software Requirements Development in the Strategic Defense Initiative Environment." *NRL Technical Report*. Washington, DC.: Naval Research Laboratory.

2.	Hayes-Roth, F., Waterman, D. A., and Lenat, D. B., 1983. *Building Expert Systems*. Reading, MA: Addison-Wesley.

3.	Harmon, P., and King, D., 1985. *Artificial Intelligence in Business: Expert Systems*. New York: John Wiley & Sons.

4.	Waterman, D. A., 1986. *A Guide to Expert Systems*. Reading, MA: Addison-Wesley.

5.	Johnson, J., 1984. "Expert Systems: For You?" *Datamation*, February, pp. 82–88.

6.	Feigenbaum, E. A., and McCorduck, P., 1983. *The Fifth Generation.* Reading, MA: Addison-Wesley.

7.	Parsaye, K., 1985. "Tutorial on Expert Systems." In *Expert Systems in Government Conference*. Washington, DC: IEEE.

8.	Liebowitz, J., 1985. *Notes on Expert Systems: A Practical Application of Artificial Intelligence*, Continuing Engineering Education Program. George Washington University, Washington, DC.

9. Davis, G. B., 1982. "Strategies for Determining Information Requirements." *IBM Systems Journal*, 21, No. 1.

10. Tversky, A., and Kahneman, D., 1974. "Judgment under Uncertainty: Heuristics and Biases." *Science*, September.

11. Silverman, B. G., 1983. "Analogy in Systems Management: A Theoretical Inquiry." In *IEEE Transactions on Systems, Man, and Cybernetics*, Vol. SMC–13, No. 6.

12. Hayes-Roth, F., Klahr, P., and Mostow, D. J., 1980. *Knowledge Acquisition, Knowledge Programming, and Knowledge Refinement*. Rand Corporation Report R–2540–NSF. San Monica, CA: Rand Corporation.

13. Schrage, M., 1985. "Artificial Intelligence." *The Washington Post*, December 1, pp. F–1, F–6.

14. Michalski, R. S., and Larson, J. B., 1978. *Selection of Most Representative Training Examples and Incremental Generation of VL1 Hyphotheses: The Underlying Methodology and the Description of Programs ESEL and AQ11*. Department of Computer Science Report UIUCDCS–R–78–867. University of Illinois at Urbana-Champaign.

15. Silverman, B. G., 1983. *The Process of Innovation (and Development): Managerial Implications of a Psychological View*. Department of Engineering Administration Report. Washington, DC: George Washington University.

16. Winston, P. H., Binford, T. O., Karz, B., and Lowry, M., 1983. "Learning Physical Descriptions from Functional Definitions, Examples, and Precedents." *MIT AI Report No. 679*. Cambridge, MA: Massachusetts Institute of Technology.

17. Winston, P. H., 1982. "Learning by Augmenting Rules and Accumulating Censors." *MIT AI Report No. 678*. Cambridge, MA: Massachusetts Institute of Technology.

18. Winston, P. H., 1981. "Learning New Principles from Precedents and Exercises: The Details." *MIT AI Report No. 632*. Cambridge, MA: Massachusetts Institute of Technology.

19. Brown, R., 1977. "Use of Analogy to Achieve New Expertise." *MIT AI–TR–403*. Cambridge, MA: Massachusetts Institute of Technology.

20. Sternberg, R. J., 1977. "Component Processes in Analogical Reasoning." *Psychological Review*, 84, No. 4.

21. Gick, M. L., and Holyoak, K. J., 1980. "Analogical Problem Solving." *Cognitive Psychology*, 12.

22. Rumelhart, D. E., and Abramson, A. A., 1973. "A Model for Analogical Reasoning." *Cognitive Psychology, 5.*

23. Carbonell, J. G., 1983. "Learning by Analogy: Formulating and Generalizing Plans from Past Experience." In *Machine Learning—An Artificial Intelligence Approach*. Tioga Publishing.

24. Reboh, R., 1979. The Knowledge Acquisition System. In *A Computer-Based Consultant for Mineral Exploration*. California: SRI International.

25. Duda, R. O., Gaschnig, J., and Hart, P., 1979. "Model Design in the Prospector Consultation System for Mineral Exploration." In *Expert Systems in the Micro Electronic Age*. Edinburgh: Edinburgh University Press.

26. Davis, R., and Lenat, D. B., 1982. *Knowledge-Based Systems in Artificial Intelligence*. New York: McGraw-Hill, Inc.

27. Software A & E, 1984. *Knowledge Engineering System: Knowledge Base Author's Reference Manual*. Arlington, VA: Software Architecture & Engineering, Inc.

28. Davis, R., 1978. "Knowledge Acquisition in Rule-Based Systems: Knowledge About Representation as a Basis for System Construction and Maintenance." In *Pattern-Directed Inference Systems*. New York: Academic Press.

29. Eliot, L. B., 1986. "Analogical Problem-Solving and Expert Systems." *EEE Expert*, 1, No. 2, Summer.

30. Boose, J. H., 1986. *Expertise Transfer for Expert System Design*. New York: Elsevier.

31. Hart, A., 1986. *Knowledge Acquisition for Expert Systems*. New York: McGraw-Hill.

32. Lenat, D., Prakash, M., and Shepherd, M., 1986. "CYC: Using Common Sense Knowledge to Overcome Brittleness and Knowledge Acquisition Bottlenecks." *The AI Magazine*, Winter.

4 | Knowledge Representation

After acquiring knowledge from the expert, the next consideration in building an expert system is deciding on the knowledge representation approach. According to Duda [1]:

> The power of the expert system lies in the specific knowledge of the problem domain, with potentially the most powerful systems being the ones containing the most knowledge.

This suggests that the knowledge base, which is the set of domain facts and heuristics, is probably the most important component of the expert system.

In deciding among knowledge representation methods to incorporate into the expert system, a good rule of thumb is to select the approach that seems most natural to the expert. In other words, the knowledge should be represented in the expert system in the same manner that the expert is using knowledge when explaining a domain or task to the knowledge engineer. For example, suppose that an expert system is being developed to determine whether one has a cold. When interviewing the "expert on colds," let's say that he explains some knowledge in the following manner:

> If one has a runny nose, watery eyes, and a sore throat, then there is a very good likelihood that the individual has a cold. Of course, this is not certain as the person might have an allergy.

This description suggests two conclusions. One conclusion is that the expert is thinking of IF-THEN or SITUATION-ACTION kinds of rules. Thus the use of production rules (which will be explained later) might be an appropriate form of representing the knowledge for that expert system. The second conclusion is that the expert is thinking in terms of probability or possibility. Such terms as "a very good likelihood" suggest that the expert system should incorporate uncertainty in this case. It turns out that, in most cases, expert system tasks involve uncertainty and Chapter 5 will describe some of the ways that an expert system can handle uncertainty.

Five major ways of representing knowledge in an expert system—predicate calculus, production or inference rules, frames, scripts, and semantic networks—will each be discussed in turn.

Predicate Calculus

Predicate calculus is a formal reasoning approach built upon formal logic that incorporates mathematical properties (transitive and associative laws). It is made up of constants (called *terms*), predicates (called *atomic formulas*), functions (called *mappings*), and logical connectives (^ for "and," v for "or," → for "implies," and ˜ for "not"). For example, the statement "All football players are big" can be expressed in predicate calculus as shown:

(ALL (X) (IF IS-A X FOOTBALL PLAYER) (BIG X))

This means for all X, if X is a football player, then X is big. Let's take another example, derived from Rich [2] and Kaisler [3], which uses predicate calculus for representing knowledge in a knowledge base. Suppose we have the following facts, with their predicate calculus representations:

1.   Harry is a man.

```
MAN(HARRY)
```

2.   Harry is a tennis player.

```
TENNISPLAYER(HARRY)
```

3.   All tennis players are athletes.

```
(FORALL X)[TENNISPLAYERS(X)  → ATHLETE(X)]
```

4.   Bob is a coach.

```
COACH(BOB)
```

5.   All athletes either obey or disobey the coach.

```
(FORALL X)[ATHLETE(X)  → OBEYANTS(X,COACH)  OR
    DISOBEY(X,COACH)]
```

6.   Everyone is loyal to someone.

```
(FORALL X)(EXISTS Y)  LOYALTS(X,Y)
```

7.   Athletes only disobey coaches they aren't loyal to.

```
(FORALL X)(FORALL Y)[ATHLETE(X)  AND  COACH(Y)  AND
    DISOBEY(X,Y)]
            → NOT  LOYALTS(X,Y)
```

8.   Harry was disobedient to Bob.

```
DISOBEDIENT(HARRY,BOB)
```

If we want to prove, "Is Harry loyal to Bob?", the following proof could be done using predicate calculus:

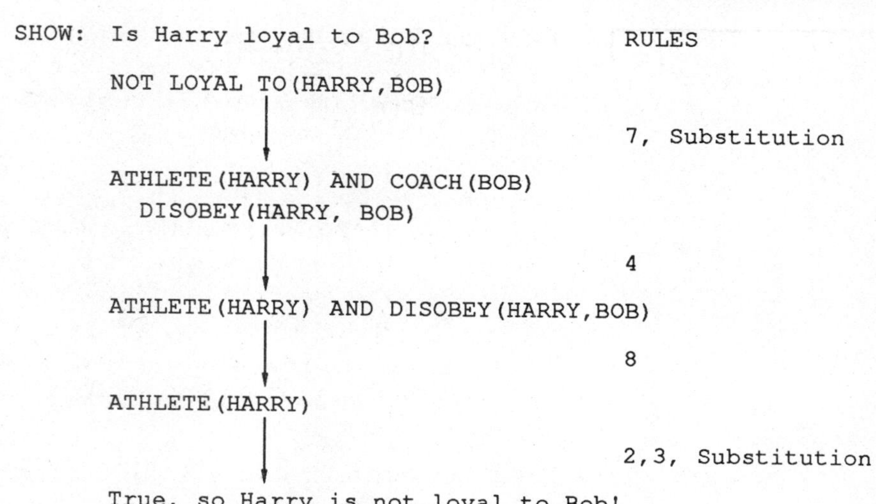

A major drawback with predicate calculus is that it provides only a skeleton of a representation scheme. Its main disadvantage is that the relevant information is not collected together, like under frames or semantic networks.

Production Rules

Another technique for representing knowledge is through production rules. This is probably the most popular approach for knowledge representation in expert systems. Production rules were popularized by Newell and Simon [4] and by Davis and King [5]. Production rules are used for representation of **procedural knowledge**—knowledge that can be executed. Production rules take the form of IF (antecedent) THEN (consequent) or SITUATION–ACTION. The rules also can have some measure of uncertainty associated with them, as will be explained in the next chapter. They have been used extensively in expert systems, particularly in expert systems used for diagnosis and planning.

A typical production rule in MYCIN, an expert system used to diagnose bacterial infections in the blood, is the following:

If:
1. The site of the culture is blood, and
2. The identity of the organism is not known with certainty, and
3. The stain of the organism is gramneg, and
4. The morphology of the organism is rod, and
5. The patient has been seriously burned,

Then:
There is weakly suggestive evidence (.4) that the identity of the organism is pseudomonas.

For the consequent of this rule to be true, each of the antecedents must be true. If one of the antecedents is false, then the consequent, using this rule, would not be concluded. Another production rule from R1, an expert system used to configure VAX computers (now called "XCON"), is shown below:

If:
1. The current context is assigning devices to unibus, and
2. There is an unassigned dual port disc drive, and
3. The type of controller it requires is known, and
4. There are two such controllers,
5. Neither of which has any devices assigned to it, and
6. The number of devices that these controllers can support is known,

Then:
Assign the disc drive to each of the controllers and note that the two controllers have been associated and that each supports one device.

According to Reggia and Perricone [6] and Software Architecture & Engineering [7], the three criteria to use in selecting a knowledge representation approach are (1) pre-existing format of the knowledge, (2) type of classification desired, and (3) context-dependence of the inference process. Production rules are usually used when the pre-existing format of the knowledge is already organized as rules, or expressed in terms of rules when the expert is explaining the task to the knowledge engineer. In this case, by using production rules, the knowledge can be kept in the same form as presently being used, thus creating an intuitive appeal [7]. Production rules are also used when the classification of knowledge is predominantly categorical. If most of the decisions in the expert system task can be answered by yes or no, then production rules would be appropriate. Last, if the knowledge has little context-dependence, then production rules are a good form for representing that knowledge because there would not be a great deal of descriptive knowledge. For descriptive knowledge, other knowledge representation methods are better, such as frames.

There are several advantages to using production rules. First, rules are a natural expression of what-to-do knowledge, i.e., procedural knowledge [3]. Second, all knowledge for a problem is uniformly presented as rules. Third, rules are comprehensible units of knowledge. Fourth, rules are modular units of knowledge, which can be easily deleted or added. Last, rules may be used to represent how-to-do knowledge, i.e., meta-knowledge. **Metaknowledge** refers to knowledge about knowledge, and can be represented as metarules. A **metarule** is a production rule that controls the application of object-level knowledge. It gives another layer of sophistication to the expert system, because it adds additional layers of spaces to a search space to help decide what to do next [8]. A disadvantage of production rules is that there is a limit on the amount of knowledge that can be expressed conveniently in a single rule [9]. This isn't a great limitation because even with using microcomputer-based expert systems shells, like EXSYS [10], a rule can have up to 126 conditions in the IF part, and up to 126 conditions in its THEN part.

Frames

A third knowledge representation method used in expert systems is frames. Frames, developed by Minsky [11] and Kuipers [12], are used for declarative knowledge. **Declarative knowledge**, as contrasted with procedural knowledge, is knowledge that can't be immediately executed but can be retrieved and stored. Frames were developed because there was evidence that people do not analyze new situations from scratch and then build new knowledge structures to describe those situations [2]. Instead, people use analogical reasoning and take a large collection of structures, available in memory, to represent previous experience with objects, locations, situations, and people [2]. According to Rich [2] frames: (1) contain information about many aspects of the objects or situations that they describe, (2) contain attributes that must be true of objects that will be used to fill individual slots, and (3) describe typical instances of the concepts they represent. Frames are used in situations where there is a large amount of context-dependence, thus implying the use of descriptive knowledge. Frames are represented like cookbook recipes, where there would be **slots filled** with the ingredients needed for the recipe, and then procedural attachments (e.g.,if-added, if-needed, and to-establish procedures) would be used to manipulate the data (i.e., to fill the slots) within and among the frames, such as to go through the steps on how actually to cook the recipe. Default values may be provided with frames. Each frame corresponds to one entity and contains a number of labeled slots for things pertinent to that entity [13]. Slots in turn may be blank, or may be specified by terminals referring to other frames, so the collection of frames is linked together into a network [13]. This allows the organization of knowledge to be useful for modularity and accessibility of the knowledge [14]. Attempts to design general knowledge structures based on the frames concept were made by Bobrow and Winograd via the Knowledge Representation Language, and by Roberts and Goldstein via the Frame Representation Language.

A special kind of frame is sometimes called a script. Clusters of facts can have useful special-purpose structures that exploit specific properties of their restricted domain [2]. A script, developed by Schank [15] in 1977, is such a structure that describes a stereotyped sequence of events in a particular context. The components of a script include the following [2,15]:

- Entry conditions.
- Results—conditions that will generally be true after the events described in the script have occurred.
- Props—slots representing objects.
- Roles—slots representing people.
- Track—specific variation on a more general pattern that is represented by a particular script.
- Scenes—actual sequences of events that occur.

Figure 4-1 is an example of part of a Restaurant Script [15]. In this script the track is a coffee shop. The entry conditions are given where the customer is hungry and has money. The scenes of entering the coffee shop, ordering, eating, and exiting are displayed. The results of this script are the customer has less money, is not hungry (hopefully!), and is pleased (optional). Another result is the owner of the coffee shop has more money. Scripts are helpful when there are many causal relationships between events [2].

Figure 4-1

Example (part of restaurant script [Schank])

Script:	Restaurant		Scene 1:	Entering
Track:	Coffee Shop		S PTRANS S into restaurant	
Props:	Tables		S ATTEND eyes to tables	
	Menu		S MBUILD where to sit	
	F=Food		S PTRANS S to table	
	Check		S MOVE S to sitting position	
	Money			
Roles:	S=Customer		Scene 2:	Ordering
	W=Waiter		.	
	C=Cook		.	
	M=Cashier		.	
	O=Owner		Scene 3:	Eating
Entry Conditions:	S is hungry.		.	
	S has money.		.	
Results:	S has less money		.	
	O has more money		Scene 4:	Exiting
	S is not hungry		.	
	S is pleased (optional)		.	

Source: Schank, R. C. and R. P. Abelson. *Scripts, Plans, Goals, and Understanding*. Erlbaum, Hillsdale, N.J. (1977). Reprinted with permission from Lawrence Erlbaum Associates, Inc., Hillsdale, New Jersey.

Semantic Networks

The last major way of representing knowledge in an expert system is by semantic networks. Semantic networks were discovered by Quillian [16] and Raphael [17] in 1968, and are used for representing declarative knowledge. With semantic networks, knowledge is organized around the objects being described, but objects are represented as nodes in a graph and relations among them are represented by labeled arcs. A semantic network is a collection of nodes and arcs where the following apply [2]:

- Nodes represent classes, objects, concepts, situations, events, etc.
- Nodes have attributes with values that describe the characteristics of the things they represent.
- Arcs represent relationships between nodes.
- Arcs allow us to organize knowledge hierarchically within a network.

For example, Figure 4-2 shows a fragment of a semantic network on computers. This figure shows the following associations:

MICROCOMPUTER	Isa	COMPUTER
DISK DRIVE	Ispart	MICROCOMPUTER
IBM PC	Isa	MICROCOMPUTER
IBM PC	Color	BEIGE
IBM PC	Isattached	OKIDATA 192
IBM PC	Owner	ME
OKIDATA 192	Isa	PRINTER
ME	Isa	PERSON

Figure 4-2

Fragment of a computer semantic network

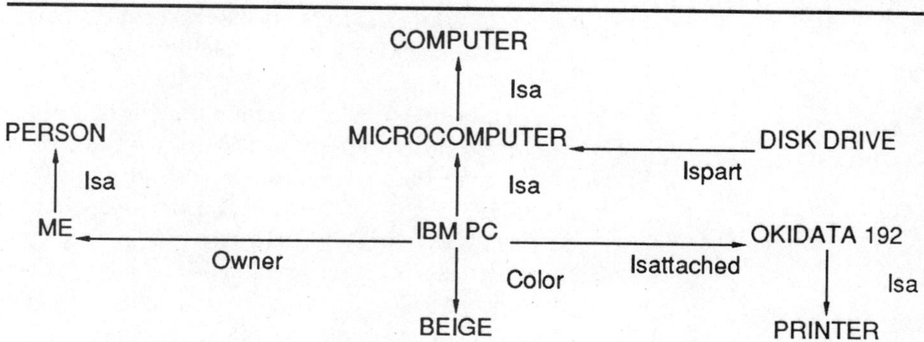

This is only a fragment of a semantic network on computers because we haven't included all the relevant nodes and arcs relating to microcomputers, nor any of those nodes and arcs associated with other kinds of computers, like minicomputers, mainframes, supermini-computers, supercomputers, and lap-size computers.

The reasoning in semantic networks depends on the procedures used to manipulate the network. The following steps are usually accomplished [2]:

- Basically, match patterns against one or more nodes to retrieve information; heuristics may be needed to tell where to begin matching.
- Inference—derive general properties by examining a set of nodes for common features and relations.
- Deduction—follow paths through a set of nodes to derive a conclusion.

The main advantage of using semantic networks is that for each object, event, or concept, all the relevant information is collected together [2]. Such networks used to represent specific events or experiences, and are used for tasks that have a large amount of context-dependence.

Case Study: READ Continued

In Chapter 3 READ's knowledge acquisition stage was discussed, which resulted in an attribute hierarchy based on interviews with the expert. The next step deals with the best way of representing the knowledge acquired from the expert.

The pre-existing format of determining command management system (CMS) software functional requirements is already organized as rules. Rules are implicitly used in the present way of developing CMS software requirements. The CMS designer thinks of rules in the IF-THEN format but does not formally list the rules. For example, the CMS designer may think this way:

If: 1. Operations support is required, and
     2. The user is a computer, or
     3. The user is an offsite principal investigator,
Then:
     Support communications to external areas.

The CMS software designers indicate that requirements for new satellites are based on previous requirements for earlier satellites in cases of similar satellite apparatus and functions. By using a **rule-based** deductive expert system prototype, the knowledge can be kept in the same form as presently being used, thus creating an intuitive appeal [7].

The second factor to be considered for knowledge representation selection is the type of classification. Classification types are typically either probabilistic, categorical, or mixed [7]. In the CMS software functional requirements domain, the classification is predominantly categorical. This can be seen as most of the decisions in the requirements determination are yes-no answers. For example, the question of needing real-time user response can be answered by yes or no. Additionally, since there are three major classes of future satellite missions, analogical reasoning can be used to categorize, under each class, previous satellite CMS requirements information. Conditional probabilities, needed for a Bayesian-probabilistic approach to classification, would be difficult to determine, in this case, due to a large volume of test data necessary to compute a priori probabilities.

The last major consideration in adopting a knowledge representation scheme is the context-dependence of the inference process. Rule-based deduction is an appropriate method for this problem domain when considering context-dependence. This is true because the number of attributes per antecedent is very low [7]. This is helpful for writing a set of rules as not all of the context for using each rule has to be included in the antecedents of the rule [7].

Based upon the aforementioned criteria, a rule-based deduction approach was used as the knowledge representation method.

After deciding on a rule-based approach, the next phase involved writing the rules based upon the attribute hierarchy and discussions with the expert. The rules, in handwritten form, were shown to the expert for their comments. Some rules had to be changed immediately due to omissions of attributes, incorrect cause-and-effect relationships, and inappropriate attribute names. Since each rule was in the form "IF antecedent THEN consequent" **<certainty factor>**, the certainty factors next needed to be determined by the expert. These certainty factors were determined by the expert's best judgment, in which values between -1.0 (absolutely false) and 1.0 (absolutely true) were assigned to the consequent of each rule, as explained in the next chapter. Figure 4-3 shows an excerpt of the 154 rules used in the expert system prototype.

Expert systems today have been able to encapture considerable amounts of expert knowledge. COMPASS, an expert system used for switch maintenance, has about 1000 frames and 500 rules. MYCIN, an expert system for diagnosing bacterial infections in the blood, has over 500 rules in its knowledge base. R1/XCON, an expert system for configuring VAX computer systems, has well over 3300 rules in its knowledge base.

Figure 4-3

*Excerpt of the rules
section of the knowledge
base (total of 154 rules)*

```
rule75 if level one functional requirements = data management,
& orbit data = present,
/ telemetry data = present,
/ scheduling data = present,
/ obc data = present,
& need for installation and verification and maintenance and security
    of data base = present,
then level two functional requirements = manage project data base
& archive data files (0.5).

rule 76 [rationale: "This is needed to know if packetization is"
"present."]
    if level one functional requirements = data management,
& telemetry data = present,
& packetization = present,
then level two functional requirements = build telemetry packages.

rule 77 if level one functional requirements = data management,
& scheduling data = present,
then circum = need to resolve conflicts and coordinate schedule data
    with attitude and mission scheduling needs (0.9).

rule78 if circum = need to resolve conflicts and coordinate schedule
    data with attitude and mission scheduling needs, then level two
    functional requirements = format ncc schedule data (0.8).

rule79 if level one functional requirements = data management,
& onboard computer utilization = present,
then level two functional requirements = maintain flight data base
    parameters (0.8)
& develop facility to maintain obc software.

rule80 if level one functional requirements = operations support,
& interactive mode = present,
& display = present,
then level two functional requirements = support executive display
    interface.

rule 81 if level one functional requirements = operations supports
& joysticking = present,
/ real time user response = present,
/ user = human,
then circum = user interface language,

rule 82 if circum = user interface language,
then level two functional requirements = support language interface.

rule 83 if level one functional requirements = operations support,
& user = computer,
/ user = offsite PIs,
then level two functional requirements = support communications to
    external areas.

rule84 if level one functional requirements = operations support,
& user feedback = present,
then level two functional requirements = provide reports (0.8).
```

  The next major stage involves knowledge programming, where encoding the knowledge base takes place. This will be discussed in the next chapter.

References

1. Duda, R. O., and Gaschnig, J. G., 1981. "Knowledge-Based Expert Systems Come of Age." *BYTE,* September.
2. Rich, E., 1983. *Artificial Intelligence.* New York: McGraw-Hill, Inc.
3. Kaisler, S. M., 1984. *Expert Systems Tutorial.* ACM Professional Development Seminar, College Park, MD.
4. Newell, A., and Simon, H. A., 1972. *Human Problem Solving.* Englewood Cliffs, NJ: Prentice- Hall.
5. Davis, R., and King, J. J., 1977. "An Overview of Production Systems." In *Machine Intelligence, 8*, eds. E. Elcock and D. Michie. Chichester, England: Horwood.
6. Reggia, J. A., and Perricone, B. T., 1982. *KMS Manual.* College Park, MD: Department of Mathematics, University of Maryland.
7. Software A & E, 1984. *Knowledge Engineering System: Knowledge Base Author's Reference Manual.* Arlington, VA: Software Architecture & Engineering, Inc.
8. Hayes-Roth, F., Waterman, D. A., and Lenat D. B., 1983. *Building Expert Systems.* Reading, MA: Addison-Wesley.
9. Davis, R., 1978. "Knowledge Acquisition in Rule-Based Systems: Knowledge about Representation as a Basis for System Construction and Maintenance." In *Pattern-Directed Inference Systems.* New York: Academic Press.
10. EXSYS, Inc., 1985. *EXSYS: Expert System Development Package Manual.* Albuquerque, NM.
11. Minsky, M. A., 1975. "Framework for Representing Knowledge." In *The Psychology of Computer Vision*, ed. P. Winston. New York: McGraw-Hill.
12. Kuipers, B. J., 1975. "A Frame for Frames." In *Representation and Understanding*, eds. D. G. Bobrow and A. Collins. New York: Academic Press.
13. Quinlan, J. R., 1984. "Fundamentals of the Knowledge Engineering Problem." In *Introductory Readings in Expert Systems*, ed. D. Michie. New York: Gordon and Breach Science Publishers.
14. Nau, D. S., 1983. "Expert Computer Systems." *IEEE Computer*, February.
15. Schank, R. C., and Abelson, R. P., 1977. *Scripts, Plans, Goals, and Understanding.* Hillsdale, NJ: Erlbaum.
16. Quillian, R., 1968. "Semantic Memory." In *Semantic Information Processing*, ed. M. Minsky. Cambridge, MA: MIT Press,.
17. Raphael, B., 1968. "A Computer Program for Semantic Information Retrieval." In *Semantic Information Processing*, ed. M. Minsky. Cambridge, MA: MIT Press.

5 Knowledge Programming

After selecting the knowledge representation method for the expert system, the next step is to encode the knowledge into the knowledge base. This is the knowledge programming phase. It is an iterative process in which knowledge is acquired, represented, programmed, and refined until the expert system's performance meets the anticipated expectations. An important part of the knowledge programming step involves the mechanism that the expert system uses to perform its inferencing. Another critical component of this programming step is the expert system's ability to handle uncertainty. This chapter will first address some inferencing procedures and then discuss some ways of handling uncertainty in expert systems. After a brief look at languages used for expert systems development, the knowledge programming stage for READ will be explained.

Inference Engine

For the expert system to generate a solution, a strategy must be used to search the knowledge base and logically arrive at a conclusion. The part of the expert system that manipulates the knowledge housed in the knowledge base to generate hypotheses is called the inference engine. Within the inference engine, various search strategies could be employed to generate solutions. An analogy can be drawn comparing a barrel of M&M candies and one's hand to the knowledge base and inference engine of an expert system, respectively. Let's say that there is a barrel of different-colored M&M candies, and someone wants to pick a green M&M from the barrel. The barrel of M&Ms might act as the knowledge base, and the inference engine might be one's hand searching through the barrel for a green M&M. Different search strategies could be used to get a green M&M. One might use plausible reasoning, and put one's hand in the barrel without looking in the barrel to *guess* the right solution (i.e., pick a green M&M). Another search strategy might be to take a handful of M&Ms from the barrel, and then search that handful for a green M&M. This might be compared to the search technique of decomposing the solution space into subproblems.

Three major methods could be used efficiently to search a space for deriving hypotheses from the knowledge base. These solution direction techniques are backward chaining, forward chaining, and forward and backward processing combined. Backward chaining, called goal-directed reasoning, is a method that entails having a goal or a hypothesis as a starting point, and then "working backwards" along some paths to see if the conclusion is true. In backward chaining, Weiss and Kulikowski [1] say this about the system:

> ...has a set of initial goals, and the rules are invoked in reverse order. The system begins by examining a limited set of production rules, whose consequents are the goals. The system then proceeds to examine the antecedents of rules to see which of the goals (consequents) are satisfied. As the rules are examined in this backward unraveling, some premises (of the antecedents of the rules) are unknown (logically unsatisfied) and therefore they become new subgoals. If a subgoal is unknown, a question may be asked to determine its status.

Figure 5-1

Inference engine (problem-processing system) of DIAGNOSE

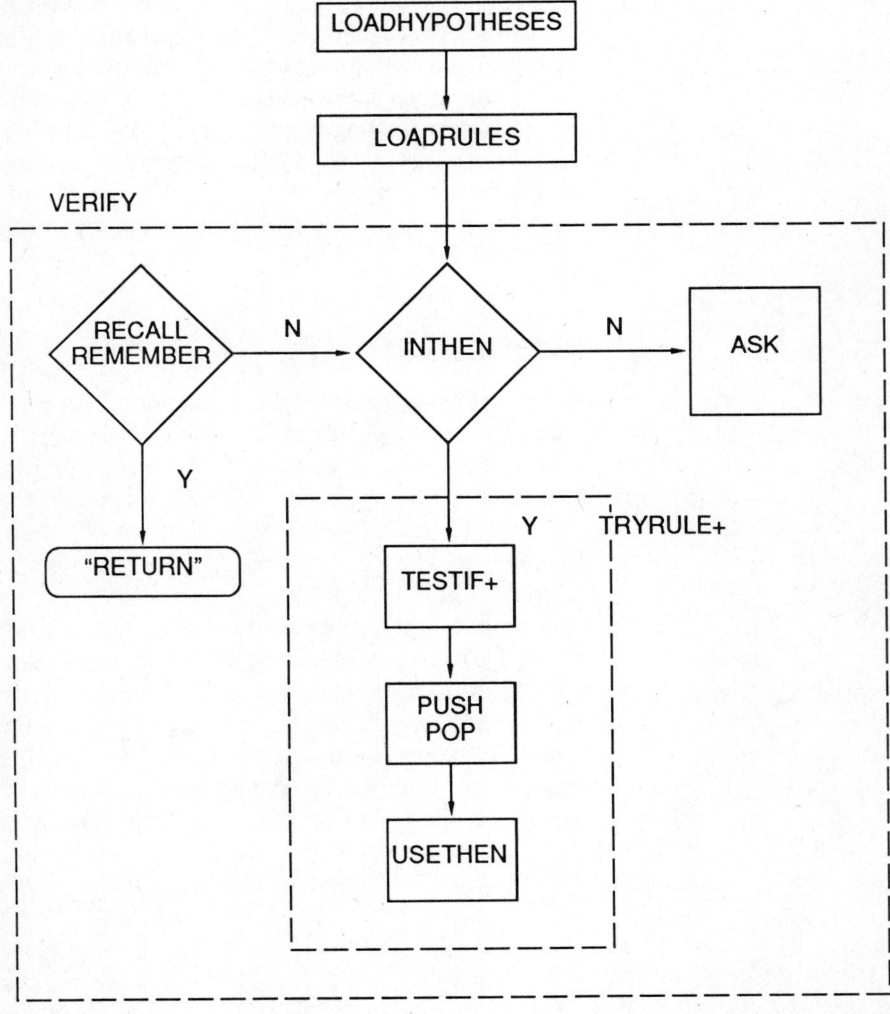

An example of backward chaining can be shown through Duda's [2] recoding of DIAGNOSE [3]. The goal of this simple rule-based expert system is to establish the truth of one of many hypotheses; in this case, the hypotheses are that an animal is either an albatross, penguin, ostrich, zebra, giraffe, tiger, or cheetah. The expert system deduces which animal the user is thinking of by asking questions based on IF-THEN data rules. This expert system consists of 426 lines of code and is written in BASIC. The inference engine consists of twelve subroutines, as shown in Figure 5-1. LOADHYPOTHESES loads the hypotheses (i.e., the animal is an albatross, penguin, etc.) into the inference engine, and LOADRULES loads the IF-THEN rules one at a time. VERIFY is then invoked, which consists of several subroutines. RECALL and REMEMBER are first invoked to see if the rule has already been asked, i.e., to test the truth of the rule. If the truth of that rule has already been determined, then the next rule is invoked to try to generate a hypothesis. If the truth of the rule hasn't been determined, IFTHEN is used to test the antecedent of the rule. TESTIF+ is then used to see if there are other rules that can determine the truth of that antecedent. If the antecedent is true, then PUSH and POP store it in a stack and USETHEN stores the consequent(s) of that rule. If there are not any rules to determine the truth of the antecedent, then ASK will ask the user if that antecedent is true.

Figure 5-2 shows an "and/or" graph, with the attributes and rules used to construct the knowledge base. These attributes and rules are derived from conversations with someone knowledgeable on animals. Rule#1 (R1), for example, shows: IF the animal has hair THEN it is a mammal. This is a modified version of an attribute hierarchy, as the rules are also depicted in this hierarchy.

Backward chaining can be demonstrated as shown in Figure 5-3. Assume that the conclusion should be that the animal is a cheetah. Through backward chaining, the expert system arbitrarily starts at a hypothesis—in this case the animal is an albatross. Rule R15, as shown in Figure 5-2, is associated with this hypothesis:

```
If:     The animal is a bird, and flies well,
Then:   The animal is an albatross.
```

To test the first antecedent (i.e., the animal is a bird), the expert system uses exhaustive search, in this case, to see if there are any rules to determine if an animal is a bird. Exhaustive search is used if a problem is small or can be broken up into small independent subproblems [4]. Here a single line of reasoning is used, and usually the data and knowledge are reliable and static. In our case two rules, R3 and R4, can determine if an animal is a bird:

```
R3:   IF     has feathers
      THEN   is bird.


R4:   IF     flies, and
             lays eggs
      THEN   is bird.
```

If there were not any rules to deduce if the animal is a bird, then the expert system would ask the user: "Is the animal a bird?" Through exhaustive search, the expert system searches its knowledge base for rules to conclude if an animal has feathers. There are no rules to infer this, so the expert system asks the user: "Is this true: the animal has feathers?" Since the animal is a cheetah, the user types "n" for no. The expert system then asks the

Figure 5-2

And/Or graph (attribute hierarchy) of DIAGNOSE —an example to under- stand better how PPS works

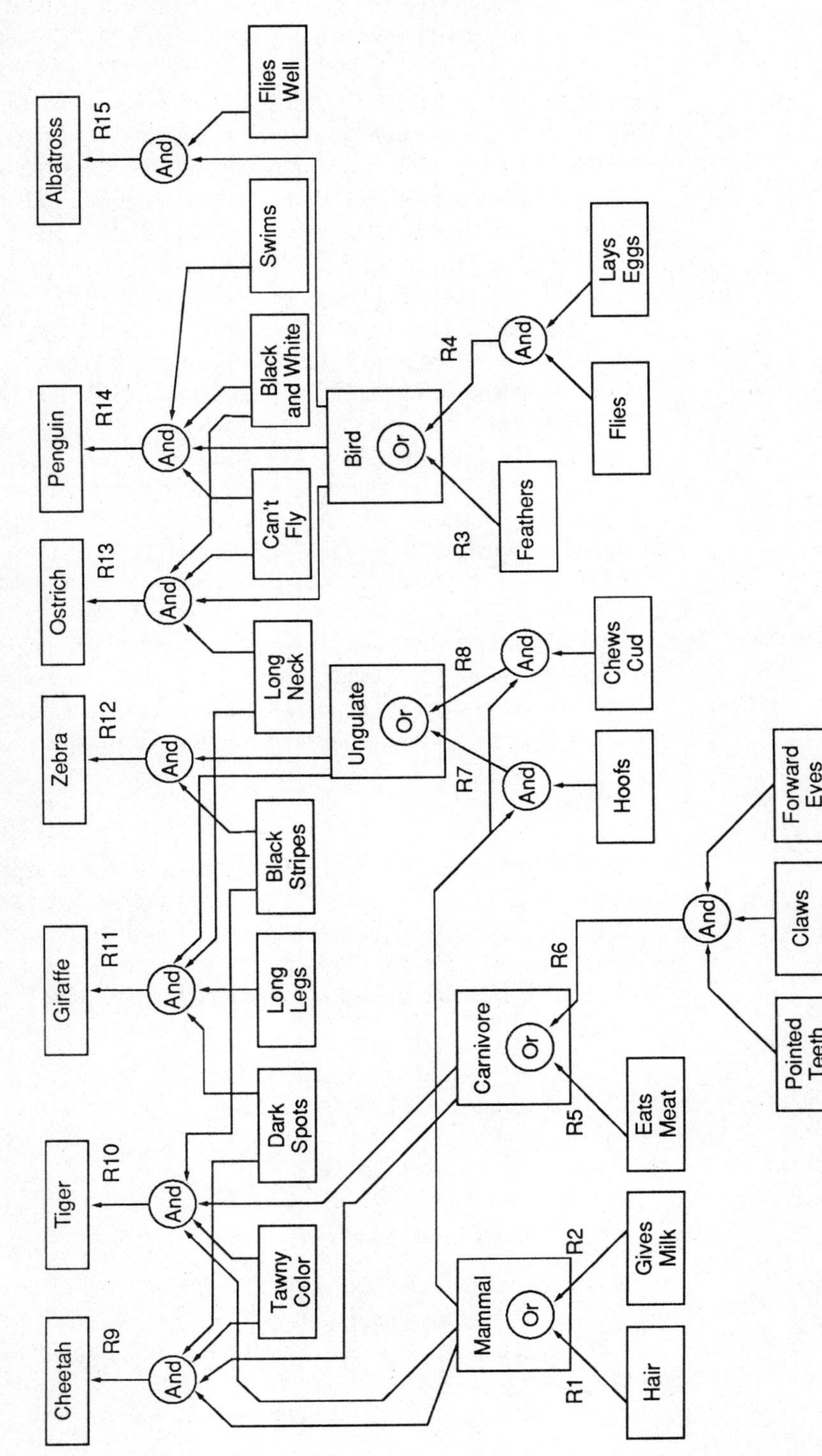

user, from rule R4 and since no other rules infer its value, "Is this true: the animal flies?" The user responds, "n". Thus, since rules R3 and R4 fail, rule R15 cannot be true because the animal cannot be a bird. Therefore, the hypothesis that the animal is an albatross fails, and the expert system considers the next hypothesis. The backward chaining process is continued as shown in Figure 5-3, and the important point to remember is that the expert system is trying to prove a hypothesis by working through the facts. Figure 5-4 shows the output from this dialogue. Of course, this simple expert system is limited due to its inability to handle uncertainty and its limited explanation capabilities.

Figure 5-3

Backward chaining process of DIAGNOSE

```
LOOKS AT FIRST HYPOTHESIS ("IS ALBATROSS")

                                                           ANSWER

R15    IF "IS BIRD", "FLIES WELL", THEN, "IS
       ALBATROSS"
       R3 IF "HAS FEATHERS", THEN, "IS BIRD"         N
       R4 IF "FLIES", "LAYS EGGS", THEN, "IS BIRD"   N
                                                     THEREFORE, NOT BIRD

R14    LOOKS AT PENGUIN (HYP.2)
R13    LOOKS AT OSTRICH (HYP.3) REJECT DUE TO IF
       "IS BIRD"...THEN...
R12    LOOKS AT ZEBRA (HYP.4)
          IF "IS UNGULATE", "HAS BLACK STRIPES",
       THEN, "IS ZEBRA"
       R7 IF "IS MAMMAL", "HAS HOOFS", THEN, "IS
       UNGULATE"
       R8 IF "IS MAMMAL", "CHEWS CUD", THEN, "IS
       UNGULATE"
       R1 IF "HAS HAIR", THEN, "IS MAMMAL"           Y MAMMAL
       R2 IF "GIVES MILK", THEN, "IS MAMMAL"

                                                     N
                                                     N NOT UNGULATE
                                                     THEREFORE, REJECT
                                                     ZEBRA DUE TO NOT
                                                     UNGULATE

R11    THEN, REJECT GIRAFFE (HYP.5) DUE TO:
          IF "IS UNGULATE"...
R10    LOOK AT TIGER (HYP.6)
          IF "IS MAMMAL", "IS CARNIVORE", "HAS
       TAWNY COLOR", "HAS BLACK STRIPES", THEN,
       "IS TIGER"
       R5 IF "EATS MEAT", THEN, "IS CARNIVORE"       Y CARNIVORE
                                                     Y TAWNY
                                                     N-NO STRIPES
                                                       THUS, NOT TIGER

R9     LOOK AT CHEETAH (HYP.7)
       IF "IS MAMMAL", "IS CARNIVORE", "HAS
       TAWNY COLOR", "HAS DARK SPOTS", THEN,
       "IS CHEETAH"

                                                     Y DARK SPOTS
              THEREFORE, ANIMAL IS A CHEETAH!
```

Figure 5-4

*Sample Output
of DIAGNOSE*

```
]RUN
HELLO.
I WILL USE MY 15 RULES TO TRY TO ESTABLISH
ONE OF THE
FOLLOWING 7 HYPOTHESES:
      ANIMALIS ALBATROSS
      ANIMALIS PENGUIN
      ANIMALIS OSTRICH
      ANIMALIS ZEBRA
      ANIMALIS GIRAFFE
      ANIMALIS TIGER
      ANIMALIS CHEETAH
PLEASE ANSWER MY QUESTIONS WITH Y (YES),
  N (NO), OR W (WHY)
IS THIS TRUE: ANIMALHAS FEATHERS?N
IS THIS TRUE: ANIMALFLIES?N
IS THIS TRUE: ANIMALHAS HAIR?Y
RULE R1 DEDUCES ANIMALIS MAMMAL
IS THIS TRUE: ANIMALHAS HOOFS?N
IS THIS TRUE: ANIMALCHEWS CUD?N
IS THIS TRUE: ANIMALEATS MEAT?Y
RULE R5 DEDUCES ANIMALIS CARNIVORE
IS THIS TRUE: ANIMALHAS TAWNY COLOR?Y
IS THIS TRUE: ANIMALHAS BLACK STRIPES?W
I AM TRYING TO USE RULE R10
I ALREADY KNOW THAT:
ANIMALIS MAMMAL
ANIMALIS CARNIVORE
ANIMALHAS TAWNY COLOR
IF:
ANIMALHAS BLACK STRIPES
THEN:
ANIMALIS TIGER
IS THIS TRUE: ANIMALHAS BLACK STRIPES?N
IS THIS TRUE: ANIMALHAS DARK SPOTS?Y
RULE R9 DEDUCES ANIMALIS CHEETAH
I CONCLUDE THAT ANIMALIS CHEETAH.
RESTART OR QUIT (R OR Q)?Q
BREAK IN 870
```

A problem with backward chaining is the handling of conjunctive subgoals [5]. In general, to attack a conjunction, one must find a case where all interacting subgoals are satisfied, a search for which can often result in a combinatorial explosion of possibilities [6]. Expert systems using backward chaining are those used mainly for diagnosis, like MYCIN, and for planning.

Forward chaining, often described as event-driven or data-directed reasoning, is a natural direction for problem solving when data or basic ideas are a starting point [5]. Forward chaining is a problem-solving paradigm in which the expert system does not start with any particular goals defined for it [1]. Instead of working from conclusions to facts, as with backward chaining, forward chaining is the opposite where the system works from facts to conclusions. It might be thought of as bottom-up reasoning, versus top-down reasoning. According to Weiss and Kulikowski. [1]:

It has no initial subgroup of production rules which establish a starting point. Instead, the system starts with a subset of evidence and proceeds to invoke the production rules in a forward direction, continuing until no further production rules can be invoked.

One possible drawback of forward chaining is that one would derive everything possible whether one needed it or not. Forward chaining has been used in expert systems for data analysis, design, diagnosis, and concept formation, like DENDRAL and HARPY.

Forward and backward processing combined is another method used for search direction in the inference engine. This approach is used when the search space is large and can be divided hierarchically, so both a bottom-up and top-down search can be appropriately combined [5]. This combined search is applicable to complex problems incorporating uncertainties, such as speech understanding (HEARSAY II) [5,7].

Two major factors must be considered when deciding upon the search direction technique. The first consideration is that the expert system should closely match the reasoning pattern that the expert uses. For example, if the expert's way of reasoning is a top-down approach, then backward chaining should probably be used. If the expert system's reasoning pattern is drastically different from the expert's, then implementation and acceptance of the expert system will be difficult. The second factor that influences the search direction technique is that the expert system should move from the smallest set of states to the largest (and thus easiest to find) set of states [8]. For example, it is generally easier to drive from an unfamiliar place to home than from home to the unfamiliar place. For this case backward reasoning should be used, where the starting position is home and the goal position is the unfamiliar (and smaller target) place, and the route should be planned by reasoning backward from the unfamiliar place. Forward reasoning might be used, however, for symbolic integration [8]. Suppose the start space is a formula containing some integral expression, and the **goal state** (i.e., desired final outcome) is a formula that is equivalent to the initial one and doesn't contain any integral expressions. This example consists of a large number of goal states. It is easier to use rules for integration to try to generate an integral-free expression than to start with an arbitrary integral-free expression, and use rules for differentiation to try to get the integral that we are trying to solve [8]. Thus, in this case, forward reasoning is appropriate because the expert system should reason from the smaller set of states to the larger set of states. Forward and backward processing combined is appealing if the number of nodes at each step grows exponentially with the number of steps that have been taken. This divide-and-conquer approach is also good for blind search to move forward from the start state and backward from the goal state simultaneously [8].

Besides the search methods mentioned, other techniques can be built into the inference engine to search a large search space and for search space transformation. These methods will be briefly mentioned below [4,5,9]:

- Generate and Test (Hierarchical)—In this approach the system generates possible solutions, and a tester prunes the solutions that fail to meet appropriate criteria (reasoning by elimination).
- Dependency-Directed Backtracking—This method traces errors and inconsistencies back to the inferential steps that created them.
- Least Commitment—Decisions are not made arbitrarily or prematurely, but are postponed until there is enough information, such as with NOAH.

- Multilines of Reasoning—Under this approach a limited number of solutions in parallel are carried through the problem solving process, until the best of the solutions is clarified, such as with SYN.
- Breaks into Subproblems—This approach dissects the search space into independent subproblems, such as with R1/XCON.
- Multiple Models—This approach uses multiple models for simplifying a search, such as with SYN.
- Constraint Propagation—This method represents interactions between subproblems as constraints, and formulates the constraints as goals to be solved, as under MOLGEN.
- Hierarchical Refinement—This method develops a high-level solution that can then be iteratively refined, successfully including more details.
- Hierarchical Resolution—This technique hierarchically divides the solution space into contributing subspaces in which the elements of the higher-level spaces are composed of elements from the lower spaces, such as with spacecraft and aircraft design.
- Dealing with Time—This method uses situations that change when sufficient actions have taken place, or when new data indicates a situational shift is appropriate, as with VM.

Inference engines can be designed to handle these search space approaches, and most of them also have the ability for reasoning in the presence of uncertainty. In many cases one must deal with uncertainty in data or in knowledge. Thus an expert system should allow for handling this uncertainty, as will be discussed next.

Dealing with Unreliable Data or Knowledge in Expert Systems

Uncertainty is a key factor in decision making. Even experts are not sure one hundred percent of the time. Under severe time pressure, experts make judgments sometimes based on unavailable data, incomplete data, or unreliable data [4]. For example, in locating a patient's primary source of cancer, a medical expert may draw inferences from uncertain data due to conflicting test results.

Most expert systems are designed to handle uncertainty. There are both formal and informal/inexact reasoning approaches to handling uncertainty.

Formal Reasoning Approach to Handling Uncertainty: Bayesian Approach

The **Bayesian statistics** approach uses Bayes' Theorem for handling an expert's uncertainty in making judgments about a certain domain. Bayes' Theorem is [10,11,12]:

```
If  H₁,  H₂,  . . . ,  Hₖ are mutually exclusive events and  A
is an event,
    P(Hᵢ/A)  =    P(Hᵢ)  P(A/Hᵢ)
                ─────────────────────
                 Σ (P(Hᵢ)  P(A/Hᵢ))
```

then $P(H_i/A)$ is the probability of H_i given A, and
$P(A/H_1)$, $P(A/H_2)$, . . . are prior probabilities.

For example [11]: 2% of a population have tuberculosis (i.e.,

```
P(T)  =  .02), and
  If:
  P(X/T)        =  probability that an X-ray of a tubercular
                   person is positive
                =  .90, and
  P(X/Not-T)    =  probability that an X-ray of a healthy
                   person is positive
                =  .01
  Then:
  P(T/X)        =  probability that a person with a positive
                   X-ray has tuberculosis
```

$$P(T/X) = \frac{P(T)\,P(X/T)}{P(T)\,P(X/T) + P(not\text{-}T)\,P(X/not\text{-}T)}$$

$$= \frac{(.02)(.90)}{(.02)(.90) + (.98)(.01)}$$

$$= .648$$

There could be problems with using Bayesian reasoning for handling uncertainty [11]: (1) the events must be disjoint; (2) prior probabilities are critical; (3) prior probabilities are often suspect or unobtainable; (4) Bayesian reasoning could lead to combinatorial explosion; and (5) a large amount of data is required to determine all of the conditional probabilities needed in Bayes' formula.

Prospector is an example of an expert system that uses Bayesian reasoning for handling uncertainty as well as using certainty scales. Prospector aids geologists in evaluating the favorability of an exploration site or region for occurrence of ore deposits of particular types [13].

Here is a typical production rule in Prospector [11]:

```
IF:      There is hornblende pervasively altered to
         biotite
THEN:    There is strong evidence (320,0.001) for
         potassic zone alteration.
```

The number 320, called the measure of sufficiency (*LS*), indicates how sufficient the evidence is for establishing the hypothesis, if the evidence is, in fact, present. The number 0.001, called the necessity measure (*LN*), indicates the degree to which the absence of this evidence will rule out the hypothesis [11]. Bayes' rule is used to determine these two numbers by the following formulas [13]:

$$\text{(1)} \quad O(H/E) = LS\,O(H)$$

$$\text{(2)} \quad LS = \frac{P(E/H)}{P(E/not\ H)}$$

$$\text{(3)} \quad O(H/not\ E) = LN\,O(H)$$

$$\text{(4)} \quad LN = \frac{P(not\ E/H)}{P(not\ E/not\ H)}$$

where:

$$O(H/E) \quad = \quad \text{the posterior odds on the hypothesis, } H \text{, given that the evidence, } E \text{, is observed to be present}$$

$$O(H) \quad = \quad \text{prior odds on the hypothesis}$$

$$LS \quad = \quad \text{measure of sufficiency}$$

$$LN \quad = \quad \text{necessity measure}$$

Values greater than 1 increase the likelihood of the sufficiency or necessity of the evidence for establishing the hypothesis, and values less than 1 decrease the likelihood [11,13]. The user expresses his/her certainty about E on an arbitrary -5 to 5 scale, where 5 denotes that the evidence is definitely present, -5 denotes that it is definitely absent, 0 indicates no information, and intermediate values denote degrees of certainty [13].

▌ Informal/Inexact Reasoning Approaches to Handling Uncertainty

Informal reasoning approaches to handling uncertainty are often necessary due to the inexact nature of the available data. The three approaches to be considered here are belief functions, the Dempster–Shafer method, and fuzzy logic.

Belief Functions   Another approach for handling an expert's uncertainty deals with **belief** functions. These functions are also called certainty or confidence factors (CF), as used, for example, in the case of MYCIN. Belief functions can be tied in with the interactions between one's value hierarchies and views. Inference bias comes primarily from these interactions. Belief functions are ways to account for and represent this bias, as shown next in the discussion of MYCIN.

MYCIN is an expert system designed to diagnose and recommend therapies for bacterial infections in the blood. MYCIN associates a certainty factor with each of its production rules. The CF indicates the certainty with which each fact or rule is believed to hold and is a number between -1 and 1 [14]. Rather than simply encoding the strength of association between symptom and cause, a certainty factor also captures how important it is that a diagnosis be considered in therapy selection [15]. Thus a frequently fatal cause of a disease would be assigned a higher certainty factor than a competing cause that is more likely, but rarely fatal.

To evaluate MYCIN's production rules, the following steps are used [14]:

- The CF of a conjunction of several facts is taken to be the minimum of the CFs of the individual facts.
- The CF of a disjunction of several facts is taken to be the maximum of the CFs of the individual facts.
- The CF for the conclusion produced by a rule is the CF of its premise multiplied by the CF of the rule.
- The CF for a fact produced as the conclusion of one or more rules is the maximum of the CFs produced by the rules yielding that conclusion.

For example, suppose MYCIN is trying to establish fact D, and the only rules concluding anything about *D* are these [14]:

```
IF  A and B and C, THEN CONCLUDE D  (CF = .8)
IF  H and I and J, THEN CONCLUDE D  (CF = .7)
```

If facts *A, B, C, H, I,* and *J* are known with *CF*s of .7, .3, .5, .8, .7, and .9, respectively, then the following computation produces a *CF* of .49 for *D* [14]:

```
IF  A and B and C,
THEN  D   (CF = .8)
   CF(A)      = .7
   CF(B)      = .3     ⟩ min = .3      ⟩ .8 x .3 = .24
   CF(C)      = .5

                                                       ⟩ max = .49

IF  H and I and J,
THEN  D   (CF = .7)
   CF(H)      = .8
   CF(I)      = .7     ⟩ min = .7      ⟩ .7 x .7 = .49
   CF(J)      = .9
```

This approach of *CF* for handling an expert's uncertainty has been quite successful. This method, however, does not seem well suited to domains requiring a great deal of complex interaction between goals, or those for which it is difficult to compose sound judgmental rules [16].

Dempster–Shafer Method   One of the major problems for using Bayesian probability in expressing uncertain subjectivity is that it doesn't effectively deal with ignorance [17]. Bayesian theory cannot distinguish between the lack of belief and disbelief because the hypothesis, *H*, requires the relation of $P(A) + P(1 - A) = 1$ [17].

The Dempster–Shafer method, on the other hand, provides a useful measure for the evaluation of subjective uncertainty. This technique develops lower and upper probabilities of a particular subset. The lower probability is called the belief function because it represents the conservative amount of probability [18,19]. This lower probability is calculated as

$$P_*(A_i) = \sum_{A_j \subseteq A_i} m(A_j),$$

that is, the sum of the Dempster–Shafer's basic probabilities confined within the subset A_i [17–19]. The upper probability is defined as follows [18,19]:

$$P^*(A_i) = 1 - P_*(\bar{A}_i)$$
$$= 1 - \sum_{A_j \subseteq A_i} m(A_j)$$

where $\bar{A}_i$ is the complement set of A_i [17]. Upper probability implies the optimistic amount of probability and is also called plausibility $Pl(A_i)$ [17]. At the final goal, the decision will be based on the lower and upper probabilities. If one is a cautious decision maker, he/she will rely on the lower probability; if optimistic, he or she will take the upper probability for the decision [17].

Fuzzy Logic   Fuzzy logic was developed by Zadeh [20], and deals with laws of inference for fuzzy sets. A fuzzy set is a set of values with corresponding possibility values as follows [4]:

```
FUZZY PROPOSITION

X is a large number

CORRESPONDING FUZZY SET

({X < 10}, .1)
({10 < X < 100}, .1)
({100 < X < 1000}, .2)
({1000 < X < 1000000}, .2)
({X > 1000000}, .4)
```

The interpretation of "X is large" is that "X might be less than 10 with possibility .1, or between 10 and 100 with possibility .1," and so on. These fuzzy values are used to characterize an imprecision denotation of the proposition [4].

Zadeh [21] believes that fuzzy logic is needed in the development of production rules and associated networks of the rules. He feels that, in many situations, the interaction between the IF-THEN rules may result in illogical and "uncrisp" reasoning. For example, given the following production rules [21]:

```
IF apartments in Paris are cheap THEN it is rare
IF rare objects THEN expensive
```

the result would be, "cheap apartments in Paris are expensive," using the transitive property. This may be considered a contradiction of terms—how could *cheap* apartments be *expensive*? This example shows that the interaction between production rules may result in uncrisp and perhaps illogical thinking.

Fuzzy sets can be used to correct misinterpretations of propositions. However, if the fuzzy set descriptions are not available, then the fuzzy logic approach can not be used [4].

Languages for Expert Systems

Over the years several languages have been used for developing expert systems. LISP (*LISt Processor*) and **PROLOG** (*PROgramming in LOGic*) are probably the most used languages in artificial intelligence applications. Other languages are utilized to a lesser extent in building expert systems. Examples of these include [30]: frame-oriented systems (FRL from MIT), production-oriented (i.e., rule-oriented) languages (OPS from Carnegie-Mellon), and an assortment of other languages like Smalltalk (from Xerox), Amord (MIT), Planner (MIT), Conniver (MIT), Fuzzy (Rutgers), ROSS (Rand Corp.), and M-Actors from Kyoto. Expert systems are also being developed in conventional programming languages like C, Ada, and FORTRAN. This section will briefly address the most commonly used languages for expert systems development—namely, LISP and PROLOG.

LISP [35] is the second oldest programming language and is the most widely used symbolic processing language in the world. Various features of LISP make it helpful in developing expert systems. First, it allows for recursion. An item is **recursive** if it includes itself, like the factorial function. LISP is recursive not only in the definition of its data structure, but also in the programming techniques it allows [31]. By allowing for the use of recursion in lists and in procedures, LISP becomes a powerful language. A second feature of LISP is that it allows for LISP programs to be used as data for another LISP program. This is a benefit because information about the properties of an object (declarative knowledge) can be integrated easily with information about what actions to perform (procedural knowledge) [31]. LISP programs can easily keep track of which instructions have been executed, which helps the expert system to explain its reasoning. A third important feature of LISP is that since it is designed as an interactive language, LISP programs can be interactive while they are executing so they can obtain any additional information needed to solve a problem. Last, since LISP has been around for thirty years, many development tools have been created for LISP that enhance the programming environment [31].

Although LISP has many advantages, there are also limitations of this language. First, there are many dialects of LISP. These include MacLisp, ZETA LISP, GC LISP, C-LISP, Franz Lisp, NIL, PSL, SCHEME, T, and Interlisp. This could become confusing in understanding and learning the language. To avoid this confusion, the thrust in recent years is to develop a standard subset of LISP, namely COMMON LISP [33]. Another disadvantage of LISP is that it requires a lot of memory. Also, partly because of the difficulty in learning the language, there are not as many proficient LISP programmers as there are proficient C programmers, for example. In spite of these limitations, LISP is still considered to be the lingua franca of artificial intelligence.

PROLOG [34] is the other most commonly used language for expert systems development. PROLOG uses predicate logic (i.e., predicate calculus) as the programming language. It was developed at the University of Marseille in 1972, and is backward inference based. Unlike such conventional languages as FORTRAN or BASIC, which are *prescriptive*, PROLOG is *descriptive*. PROLOG consists of rules and facts. This suggests an important feature of logic programming, which is the separation of goals from the statements of how to satisfy them [32]. This reification of goals allows new methods to be added without the need to change the goal statements. This is very helpful in incrementally developing the expert system. Advocates of PROLOG feel that PROLOG is an easier language to learn than LISP, and that it doesn't require as much memory as needed for LISP. However, advocates of LISP feel that LISP offers more flexibility than PROLOG, and nicer programming environments have been built for LISP.

It appears that, generally speaking, the Japanese and Europeans favor PROLOG, and LISP is favored in the United States. This is partly because of where the languages were developed. An active movement in the corporate sector of the United States is to use C for expert systems development. Two factors influence this movement [36]: (1) operational concerns about the performance, power, and memory required by AI applications, and (2) availability concerns about hardware, skilled AI programmers, cost, and the integration of AI applications into mainframe corporate information systems. Many expert system companies are developing expert system applications and expert system shells in C. However, both LISP and PROLOG, are still actively used for many expert system applications, and LISP is still used for most basic research in the artificial intelligence community.

Instead of developing an expert system programmed in one of these languages, many knowledge engineers use expert system shells, particularly for prototyping of expert systems. An expert system shell is a tool for helping build expert systems. These shells will be explained in the next chapter.

It is now time to revisit READ and explain the way it handles uncertainty and discuss its knowledge programming step.

Case Study: Handling Uncertainty in READ

To determine functional requirements for command management system (CMS) software design, it seems that the Bayesian approach would be inappropriate for handling the expert's uncertainty. One of the problems with using Bayes' rule in the CMS environment is that a large amount of data would have to be collected and analyzed to determine all of the conditional probabilities needed in the formula. Part of the difficulty is the long time required to determine the probabilities of each software functional requirement needed, based upon a certain set of satellite and command management-related characteristics. Even if the conditional probabilities could be calculated, the a priori probabilities of selecting the functional requirements may be unobtainable. For example, if a new satellite has onboard technologies that never existed in previous satellites, then the functional requirements needed for the new satellite's CMS may not have a priori probabilities associated with them. Another problem with using Bayesian statistics in the CMS environment is that events may not be disjoint; thus this violates the independency between events and the mutual exclusiveness of hypotheses that are needed to implement Bayes' rule.

As an alternative to Bayesian statistics, fuzzy logic could be used to handle uncertainty in CMS functional requirements determination. It is an approximate reasoning process that is compatible with human intuitions [17]. It can yield a plausible answer even in the problems in which the conditions required for the mathematical approaches (like Bayes' Rule and Dempster–Shafer's Method) are not satisfied. A potential problem, however, does exist in using fuzzy logic. This relates to the possible difficulty in ascertaining all fuzzy set descriptions needed for each proposition.

The certainty factors approach is the preferred method for the CMS software requirements environment. It represents and utilizes judgmental knowledge in the CMS environment where (a) statistical data is lacking, (b) inverse probabilities are not known, and (c) conditional independence can be assumed in most cases [22]. It also seems intuitively appealing since it states that evidence that supports a hypothesis disfavors the negation of the hypothesis to an equal extent. Certainty factors are also useful in representing uncertainty in possibilistic terms, instead of in probabilistic values [23]. Certainty factors can be used in the CMS environment because experience with CMS software designers has shown that CMS designers do not use the information as implemented standard statistical methods [24,25]. The concept of certainty factors does appear to fit the CMS designers' reasoning patterns—their judgments of how they weigh factors, strong or weak, in decision making.

Knowledge Engineering System (KES) [27] is an expert system shell that was used to implement READ. Expert system shells will be explained in Chapter 6. It should be noted that the version of KES used in this case study is version 1.3. Newer and more powerful versions of KES have since been developed. KES uses certainty factors, similar to MYCIN, to handle uncertainty in its production rule subsystem (KES.PS). A certainty factor (*cf*) is a number between -1.0 and 1.0 that is associated with a KES.PS statement and that indicates the belief about the truth of that statement [26]. A *cf* of 1.0 means that an individual is certain that the consequent is absolutely true, given that the antecedents are true, and a *cf* of -1.0 means that one is certain that a statement is absolutely false when the antecedents are true. Values between -1.0 and 1.0 provide a measure of belief or disbelief about a statement [26]. The expert usually supplies these certainty factors as associated with each rule. For example, given the following rule:

```
rule44
if level one functional requirements=mission
   scheduling and planning,
& user feedback=present,
then circum=need scheduling reports
   and command requests for command
   loading <0.9>,
```

this means that if the antecedents are true, then there is strong evidence (0.9) that scheduling reports and command requests for command loading are needed. If a *cf* is not specified in a consequent statement, then the default value for that statement is 1.0. Also, if the attribute referred to in an antecedent has a status of Unknown, then the *cf* of that antecedent is taken to be 1.0 [26].

If there is more than one applicable rule containing the same consequent statement, KES.PS keeps track of both the cumulative evidence "for" a certain value of an attribute (*mb* or "measure of belief") and the evidence "against" this belief (*md* or "measure of disbelief") [26]. The values *mb* and *md* always lie between 0.0 and 1.0 for a particular value, where the net belief or *cf* of the value is *mb* minus *md*.

During the evaluation of rules [26]:

if an attribute already has a certain value with some *mb* and *md* and a new rule assigns the same value to that attribute with a consequent strength s 0, then the resultant *mb* and *md* are

$$mb = s * (1 - mb) + mb$$
$$md = \text{unchanged.}$$

Similarly, if $s < 0$,

$$mb = \text{unchanged,}$$
$$md = (-s) * (1 - md) + md.$$

In the case of a conjunction of antecedent statements, rule evaluation stops looking at the antecedents as soon as it finds a statement with a *cf* < 0. The rule would fail because one of the antecedents would be false, and the truth of the rule could be established only if all the antecedents (for a "conjunction") were true. For a disjunction of antecedents, rule evaluation stops when it finds a statement with a cf=1.0. It does this because a cf=1.0 represents the maximum tally possible [26].

Related to READ, if rule 102 were being evaluated:

```
rule102
  if level two functional requirements=
    verify science and mission operations,
  & safety considerations=present,
  & availability of detailed science and
    mission operations data=absent,
  then level three functional requirements=
    support scientific instrument readout,
```

and the user had already answered that the availability of detailed science and mission operations data was *present*, then this rule would fail because not all of the antecedents would be true, as needed in the case of a conjunction of antecedents. Since antecedent statements are evaluated in the same order that they were originally written, the knowledge engineer can partially control the order by consistently ordering rule antecedents in the order desired by the knowledge engineer [26].

The knowledge engineer for READ developed the order so that a level one functional requirement would trigger, if applicable, a level two functional requirement, which in turn would trigger, if applicable, a level three functional requirement. The first antecedent of a rule pertains to one of the levels of functional requirements, and it was placed in that order so the rule could be evaluated for failure at the first antecedent (in most cases) instead of waiting until the second or third antecedent statement. For example, in rule 102, if a first-level requirement did *not* generate the second-level requirement "verify science and mission operations," then rule 102 would fail at the first antecedent statement. If "verify science and mission operations" were placed as the second or third antecedent in rule 102, then the other antecedents (safety considerations and/or availability of detailed science and mission operations data) would be evaluated before getting to the evaluation of "level two functional requirements=verify science and mission operations." This would prolong the determination of the failure of rule 102.

READ: Encoding the Knowledge

An important part of the knowledge programming step is to encode the knowledge base. This step involves creating a knowledge base using a text editor and storing the knowledge base in a file in the computer's memory [28,29]. Once coded, the knowledge base is submitted by the knowledge engineer to the inference engine, which typically parses it to create objects that can be operated on by LISP codes, for example, and to check for errors, much as a compiler examines a high-level language [29].

In encoding the knowledge for READ, a file was created via the use of the UNIX editor. In this file the knowledge for the appropriate KES sections—certification, attachments, references, attributes, rules, and actions—was encoded.

The *certification* section, as shown in Figure 5-5, indicates the knowledge engineer, the dates of knowledge base development and testing procedures, and special acknowledgements. When "display certification" is entered, the contents of the certification section are displayed to the end-user; otherwise, the message "this is an uncertified knowledge base" is displayed [26]. It should be realized, however, that each expert system shell has its own unique commands and procedures for encoding the knowledge base and activating the expert system. The procedures mentioned here are applicable for the expert system shell KES.

Figure 5-5

*Certification, attachments,
and references sections
of the knowledge base*

```
certification:
 "This knowledge base is developed by Jay Liebowitz, a doctoral candidate"
 "at George Washington University.  It was developed through discussions"
 "with the domain experts, Patricia Lightfoot of NASA Goddard and Tom Pfarr"
 "of Computer Sciences Corporation over the course of eight months and was"
 "finalized in May 1984.  This knowledge base has been tested using backcasting"
 "of NASA-supported satellites ST, SMM, and DE.  These three satellites are"
 "typical of future classes of NASA satellites."
 "Special thanks and deep appreciation are extended to Patricia Lightfoot"
 "of NASA Goddard for taking so much time out of her busy schedule to aid"
 "in the development of the knowledge base.  Great thanks are also due to"
 "Software A&E, Inc. for the use of KES and the VAX computer"  %

attachments:  synonyms explain rationale question
%

references:
 "This knowledge base is built with the aid of the following references:"
 "(1) Lengthy discussions with Patricia Lightfoot of NASA Goddard and Tom"
 "Pfarr of Computer Sciences Corporation, October 1983-May 1984."
 "(2) Rogers, W.C., A CMS Classification Scheme, ORI Corporation, NASA"
 "Contract No. NAS5-26183, October 15, 1980."
 "(3) Computer Sciences Corporation, Space Telescope POCC Applications"
 "Software Support-Functional Requirements, NASA Contract NAS5-26685,"
 "July 1983."
 "(4) Costa, S.R., Ground Systems Considerations for Projects, NASA"
 "Goddard, January 1981."
 "(5) Computer Sciences Corporation, Solar Maximum Mission CMS Requirements"
 "Document, June 30, 1978."
 "(6) Computer Technology Associates, Inc., Conceptual Design for a"
 "Transportable Distributed Command and Control System:  Design Concept"
 "Document, NASA Contract NAS5-27300, October 7, 1983."
 "(7) Computer Sciences Corporation, Updates to Dynamics Explorer-A"
 "and -B CMS Requirement Definitions, NASA Contract NAS5-24300,"
 "June 1980"  %
```

The *attachments* section, shown in Figure 5-5, follows the certification section. The attachments section allows the knowledge engineer to use free-text attachments for providing definitions, synonyms, calculations, explanations, and questions of an attribute or attribute value. These free-text comments facilitate better understanding and readability on the part of the user due to enhanced explanation and interaction facilities.

The next section included in READ's knowledge base is the *references* section. This section allows the knowledge engineer to cite any sources used to develop the knowledge base. Figure 5-5 shows the contents of the references section used in READ's knowledge base. This section, as well as the certification section, is optional for inclusion in a knowledge base. When "display references" is used, the references are displayed to the end-user.

Following the references section in READ's knowledge base is the mandatory *attributes* section. This section must be included in a knowledge base, and serves in declaring the attributes shown in the attribute hierarchy (as explained in Chapter 3 and shown in Appendix A) and any associated optional attachments (synonyms of attributes) [26]. All attributes in the attribute hierarchy must be included in the attributes section. Each attribute declaration has a name, type, and value set. A name is a collection of up to 30 words, each separated by a blank space [26]. The type of an attribute can be any of the following:

(sgl)   for an attribute having only a single value at any one time
(mlt)   for multiple values at one time
(val)   for values of "present" or "absent"
(real)
(num)   } for numeric attributes
(int)

An attribute's value set refers to the possible values that an attribute can take on. Figure 5-6 shows an excerpt of the attributes included in READ's knowledge base.

Figure 5-6

*Excerpt of the attributes
section of the know-
ledge base*

```
attributes:
NCC resources [explain:  "Refers to scheduling via the Network Control Center."] (sgl):
   absent, present.
user needs for certain observations [explain:  "Refers to the experimenters having"
"needs to observe various phenomena."] (sgl):  absent, present.
pointer mission (sgl):  absent, present.
scanner mission (sgl):  absent, present.
user feedback (sgl):  absent, present.
need for wheel speeds (sgl):  absent, present.
need for power profile report (sgl):  absent, present.
need for constraint checking function (sgl):  absent, present.
onboard computer coordination work [explain:  "Refers to software needed to integrate"
"onboard computers."] (sgl):  absent, present.
user (mlt):  human, computer, offsite PIs.
orbit data (sgl):  absent, present.
need for data dissemination to different applications (sgl):  absent,
present.telemetry data (sgl):  absent, present.
scheduling data (sgl):  absent, present.
obc data (sgl):  absent, present.
need for installation and verification and maintenance and security of data base (sgl):
   absent, present.
packetization (sgl):  absent, present.
interactive mode [explain:  "Refers to the experimenter's need for interactive support."]
   (sgl):  absent, present.
display [explain:  "Refers to the experimenter's need for displaying output."] (sgl):
   absent, present.
```

Figure 5-6

(continued)

```
human interface [explain:  "Refers to need for having an input unit so the human"
" understands."] (sgl):  absent, present.
ST unique {explain:  "Refers to features, such as control sensors, that are unique to ST."]
   (sgl):  absent, present.
move spacecraft [explain:  "Refers to moving the spacecraft by, for example, jets."] (sgl):
   absent, present.
selecting a target star (sgl):  absent, present.
spacecraft constraints [explain:  "Refers to spacecraft and celestial constraints, such as"
"the spacecraft being occulted by the moon or earth."] (sgl):  absent, present.
uses TDRS (sgl):  absent, present.
availability of detailed science and mission operations data
[explain:  "Refers to the generation of detailed science and mission operations data and"
"its accessibility to CMS."] (sgl):  absent, present.
mission timeline (sgl):  absent, present.
user aid [explain:  "Refers to developing an aid for the user if the user wants. For"
"example, to execute a set of commands."] (sgl):  absent, present.
solar array positioning (sgl):  absent, present.
human input [explain:  "Refers to the existence of human input in CMS activities."] (sgl):
   absent, present.
prespecified group of commands to be executed in set sequence (sgl):  absent, present.
english of command translated into bits (sgl):  absent, present.
want english and bit configuration (sgl):  absent, present.
sensor loads to be generated (sgl):  absent, present.
real time commanding (sgl):  absent, present.
humans want translation of bits back into english (sgl):  absent, present.
memory image (sgl):  absent, present.
input data is part of telemetry stream [explain:  "Refers to the telemetry process."] (sgl):
   absent, present.
need set of limits [explain:  "Refers to the telemetry process."] (sgl):  absent, present.
historical record (sgl):  absent, present.
sophistication of mission operations staff (sgl):  complex, average, simple.
immediate feedback [explain:  "Refers to the control center operator's need for immediate"
"feedback."] (sgl):  absent, present.
online operation (sgl):  absent, present.
offline operation (sgl):  absent, present.
onsite science operations center (sgl):  absent, present.
historical fashion (sgl):  absent, present.
online communications with CMS (sgl):  absent, present.
communication on demand (sgl):  absent, present.
ref [question:  "Would you like to see the references that aided in formulating this"
"prototype"] (sgl):  yes, no.
menu [question:  "What do you want to do now"] (mlt):
   get a justification of the first level requirements reached by the requirements aid
   [synonyms:  justification],
   continue to obtain the second and third level requirements [synonyms:  advance],
   determine requirements for another satellite [synonyms:  another],
   stop--I am finished [synonyms:  halt].
```

The *rules* section, another mandatory section in READ's knowledge base, follows the attributes section. The rules are in the following form:

```
if antecedent(s) then consequent(s) <certainty factors>.
```

Figure 4-3 showed an excerpt of the 154 rules used in READ, as developed through the discussions and iterative rule refinements with the domain experts. The antecedents and consequents are made up mainly of statements, like "nature of mission=commandable." Logical connectors (& for "and", / for "or") can be used for separating antecedent statements, where disjunction has precedence over conjunction [26]. The certainty factors, as explained earlier, range from -1.0 to 1.0, where -1.0 means absolutely false and 1.0 means absolutely true. The certainty factors in the rules section are developed by the domain expert's best judgment, and they can easily be changed if needed.

The last section in READ's knowledge base, as in all KES knowledge bases, is the *actions* section. Through the actions section, the knowledge engineer can directly influence the operation of the expert system [26]. This can be achieved by including commands in the actions section. Figure 5-7 shows the actions section of READ's knowledge base, in which various commands (e.g., askfor, obtain, display) are used to control the execution of the expert system. Also, messages can be included in the knowledge base and would then be displayed to the end-user to make the expert system easier to use. The actions section must be included in a KES knowledge base.

Figure 5-7

Actions section of the knowledge base

```
actions:
display certification.
display references.
message " "
    "                       Welcome to"
    "                          the"
    "       Software Functional Requirements Aid"
    " "
    "This is an expert system prototype to help determine"
    "software functional requirements for command management"
    "activitiesof future NASA satellites."
    " "
    "Kindly answer the multiple choice questions by typing in the"
    "number associated with the response.  If 'present' appears in"
    "your set of multiple answers and is applicable to your response,"
    "then always select the response 'present' along with any other"
    "applicable responses.  For multiple answers, use the symbols '&'"
    "for 'and' and '/' for 'or', such as '1&3'."
    " "
    "If you are not sure of an answer, type either 'unknown' or type"
    "the number of the appropriate answer and indicate your certainty"
    "factor.  In the former case of typing 'unknown', This expert"
    "system prototype will generate the command management system"
    "(CMS) software functional requirements based only upon your"
    "'known' answers.  In the latter case"
    "of typing the number of the appropriate answer and indicating"
    "your certainty factor, this allows you to respond to an answer"
    "even if you are not sure of the answer.  The certainty factor is"
    "your measure of belief in the answer and can be inclusively from"
    "-1.0 (absolutely false) to 1.0 (absolutely true).  For example,"
    "if number 1 was the applicable answer but you were not"
    "absolutely positive, you could type '1 (0.5)', where 1 is your"
    "answer with a certainty factor of 0.5."
```

Figure 5-7

(continued)

```
            " "
            "If you want to know the reasons why a particular value(s) was"
            "assigned to a characteristic, then type 'justify characteristic'"
            "or type 'justify characteristic = value'.  For example, if you"
            "want to know why a pointer mission takes on a value of"
            "'present', then you would type 'justify pointer mission ="
            "present'.  After typing the justify command, type 'continue' to"
            "continue processing."
            " "
            " "
            "If none of the answers apply, type 'none'.  To terminate your"
            "session, type 'stop'.  To use this expert system prototype for"
            "another session, type 'next case'.  For other commands, type"
            "'help commands'."
            " "
            " "
            "Please type 'continue' to begin.".
    pause.
    mark.
    obtain nature of mission.
    message   "If you don't understand what the question means, typ "
              "'explain.'  If you don't understand what one of the answers"
              "of the questions means, type 'explain X', where X refers to"
              "the number corresponding to the answer.  For example, if the"
              "question reads--'safety considerations: (1) complex, (2)"
              "average, and (3) simple' and you don't understand what"
              "complex means, you would type 'explain 1'.  If there are no"
              "explanations available, this will be told to you.".
    obtain multinumber of experiments and subsystems.
    obtain coupling and interrelationships between experiments.
    obtain adaptability of payloads.
    obtain real time user response.
    obtain safety considerations.
    obtain concern with capacity of data links and line speeds and volume
        of data.
    obtain ease of scheduling.
    obtain scheduling frequency update required.
    obtain ground system architecture.
    obtain orbital position.
    obtain orbital events.
    obtain data interface.
    obtain command repertoire and syntax and attributes.
    obtain basic attitude and maneuver requirements.
    obtain control system sensors.
    obtain user interaction for command requests.
    obtain command execution conditions.
    obtain onboard computer utilization.
    obtain frequency of user output product interfacing.
    obtain target planning aids.
    obtain command sequencing planning aids.
    obtain instrument management aids.
    obtain initial orbits.
    obtain spacecraft subsystem contingencies.
    obtain special viewing periods.
    obtain simulator.
```

```
obtain user independence.
obtain data security.
obtain joysticking.
obtain user assistance and knowledge.
message " "
        "These are the major characteristics influencing CMS software"
        "functional requirements determination for a new satellite."
        "Each characteristic will now be displayed along with its"
        "associated value(s) and certainty factor(s)."
        "The certainty factor ranges inclusively from -1.0"
        "(absolutely false) to 1.0 (absolutely true), and its"
        "default value is 1.0.".
message "multinumber of experiments and subsystems:".
display value(multinumber of experiments and subsystems).
message "coupling and interrelationships between experiments:".
display value(coupling and interrelationships between experiments).
message "adaptability of payloads:".
display value(adaptability of payloads).
message "real time user response:".

display value(real time user response).
message "safety considerations:".

display value(safety considerations).
message "concern with capacity of data links and line speeds and"
"volume of data:".
display value(concern with capacity of data links and line speeds and
        volume of data).
message "ease of scheduling:".
display value(ease of scheduling).
message "scheduling frequency update required:".
display value(scheduling frequency update required).
message "ground system architecture:".
display value(ground system architecture).
message "orbital position:".
display value(orbital position).
message "orbital events:".
display value(orbital events).
message "data interface:".
display value(data interface).
message "command repertoire and syntax and attributes:".
display value(command repertoire and syntax and attributes).
message "basic attitude and maneuver requirements:".
display value(basic attitude and maneuver requirements).
message "control system sensors:".
display value(control system sensors).
message "user interaction for command requests:".
display value(interaction for command requests).
message "command execution conditions:".
display value(command execution conditions).
message "onboard computer utilization:".
display value(onboard computer utilization).
message "frequency of user output product interfacing:".
display value(frequency of user output product interfacing).
message "target planning aids:".
```

Figure 5-7

(continued)

```
display value(target planning aids).
message "command sequencing planning aids:".
display value(command sequencing planning aids).
message "instrument management aids:".
display value(instrument management aids).
message "initial orbits:".
display value(initial orbits).
message "spacecraft subsystem contingencies:".
display value(spacecraft subsystem contingencies).
message "special viewing periods:".
display value(special viewing periods).
message "simulator:".
display value(simulator).
message "user independence:".
display value(user independence).
message "data security:".
display value(data security).
message "joysticking:".
display value(joysticking).
message "user assistance and knowledge:".
display value(user assistance and knowledge).
obtain level one functional requirements.
message " "
        "These are the level one CMS software functional requirements,"
        "and respective certainty factors, for the new satellite.".
display value(level one functional requirements).
if number(level one functional requirements) = 0
then
message "By responding 'unknown' to all the aforementioned questions,"
"no 1st, 2nd, and 3rd level reqs can be generated.",
message "Therefore, you are being exited from the expert system.",
stop.
askfor ref.
if ref = yes
then
display references,
askfor menu.
if ref = no
then
askfor menu.
if menu = justification
then
message "If you would like further amplification of the justification"
"simply type 'display rationale (rule name)' where rule name is the "
"one indicated below.  To display the rule itself, typ 'display (rule"
"name)';.."
        " "
        "The following are the justifications for the first level"
        "requirements that were reached:",
justify level one functional requirements,
obtain level two functional requirements.
if menu = advance
then
obtain level two functional requirements.
if menu = another
```

Figure 5-7

(continued)

```
then next case.
if menu = halt
then stop.
message " "
            "These are the level two CMS software functional"
            "requirements, and respective certainty factors, for the new"
            "satellite.".
display value(level two functional requirements).
if number(level two functional requirements) = 0
then
message "By answering 'unknown' to all questions after the 1st level"
"reqs, no 2nd and 3rd level reqs can be generated.",
message "Therefore, you are being exited from the expert system.",
stop.
askfor carte.
if carte = just
then
message "If you would like further amplification of the justification"
"simply type 'display rationale (rule name'); where"
            "rule name is the one indicated below.  To display the rule"
            "itself, type 'display (rule name)'."
            " "
            "The following are the justifications for the second level"
            "requirements that were reached:".
justify level two functional requirements.
obtain level three functional requirements.
if carte = adv
then
obtain level three functional requirements.
if carte = anot
then next case.
if carte = hal
then stop,
message " "
            "These are the level three CMS software functional"
            "requirements, and respective certainty factors, for the new"
            "satellite.".
display value(level three functional requirements).
if number(level three functional requirements) = 0
then
message "By answering 'unknown' to all questions after the 2nd level"
"reqs, no 3rd level can be determined.",
message "Therefore, you are being exited from the expert system.",
stop.
askfor end.
if end = yes
then
message "If you would like further amplification of the justification"
"simply type 'display rationale (rule name)': where"
            "rule name is the one indicated below.  To display the rule"
            "itself, type 'display (rule name)';."
            " "
            "The following are the justifications for the third level"
            "requirements that were reached:",
```

Figure 5-7

(continued)

```
justify level three functional requirements,
message "Thanks for using this functional requirements aid.  Type"
"'next case' if you want to repeat the above with another satellite or"
"type 'stop' if you want to terminate the session.".
if end = no
then
message " "
        "Thanks for using this functional requirements aid.  Type"
        "'next case' if you want to repeat the above with another"
        "satellite or type 'stop' if you want to terminate the"
        "session." %
```

Besides the aforementioned sections in the KES knowledge base, quotations and instruction sections can be optionally included in a knowledge base. The *quotations* section allows defining one time a free-text string that is used repetitively throughout the knowledge base [26]. The *instruction* section is a separate section used to generate free-text instructions to the end-users on how to operate the expert system. Instructions can also be provided via messages in the actions section, as done in the case of READ.

To enter KES sections in a knowledge base, the knowledge engineer used the UNIX operating system although VMS could also have been used. Through UNIX, the knowledge base could be built and edited for corrections in spelling, KES syntax, and knowledge refinement. Appendix B shows an annotated user sample session with READ.

References

1. Weiss, S. M., and Kulikowski, C. A., 1984. *A Practical Guide to Designing Expert Systems.* Totowa, NJ: Rowman & Allanheld.

2. Duda, R. O., and Gaschnig, J. G., 1981. "Knowledge-Based Expert Systems Come of Age." *BYTE*, September.

3. Winston, P. H., and Horn, B. K. P., 1981. *LISP*. Reading, MA: Addison-Wesley.

4. Stefik, M., Aikins, J., Balzer, R., Benoit, J., Birnbaum, L., Hayes-Roth, F., and Sacerdoti, E., 1983. "The Architecture of Expert Systems." In *Building Expert Systems*, eds. F. Hayes-Roth, D. A. Waterman, and D. B. Lenat. Reading, MA: Addison-Wesley.

5. Gevarter, W. B., 1982. *An Overview of Expert Systems*. Washington, DC: National Aeronautics and Space Administration.

6. Buchanan, B. G., 1976. *Problem Solving with Uncertain Knowledge*. Department of Computer Science Report, Stanford University.

7. Erman, L. D., 1980. "The HEARSAY-II Speech-Understanding System: Integrating Knowledge to Resolve Uncertainties." *Computing Surveys,* 12, No. 2.

8. Rich, E., 1983. *Artificial Intelligence*. New York: McGraw-Hill, Inc.

9. Winston, P. H., and Brown, R. H., 1979. *Artificial Intelligence: An MIT Perspective*. Vol. I. Cambridge, MA: MIT Press.

10. Lindley, D. V., 1984. "The Probability Approach to the Treatment of Uncertainty in Artificial Intelligence and Expert Systems." In *Proceedings of The Calculus of Uncertainty in Artificial Intelligence and Expert Systems Conference*. Washington, DC: George Washington University.

11. Gibbons, G. D., 1982. *Knowledge-Based Systems.* Berlin Continuing Engineering Education Program, George Washington University, Washington, DC.

12. Freund, J. E., and Williams, F. J., 1972. *Elementary Business Statistics.* Englewood Cliffs, NJ: Prentice-Hall.

13. Duda, R. O., Gaschnig, J. G., and Hart, P., 1979. "Model Design in the Prospector Consultant System for Mineral Exploration." In *Expert Systems in the Micro Electronic Age*, ed. D. H. Michie. Edinburgh: Edinburgh University Press.

14. Nau, D. S., 1983. "Expert Computer Systems." *IEEE Computer*, February.

15. Clancey, W. J., 1983. "The Epistemology of a Rule-Based Expert System." *Artificial Intelligence Journal,* 20, No. 3.

16. Davis, R., Buchanan, B., and Shortliffe E., 1977. "Production Rules as a Representation for a Knowledge-Based Consultation Program." *Artificial Intelligence Journal,* 8, No. 1.

17. Ishizuka, M., Fu, K. S., and Yao, J. T. P., 1981. *Inference Procedure with Uncertainty for Problem Reduction Method.* Lafayette, IN: Purdue University, Department of Computer Science Report.

18. Dempster, A. P., 1967. "Upper and Lower Probabilities Induced by a Multivalued Mapping." *Annals of Mathematical Statistics,* 38.

19. Shafer, G., 1976. *A Mathematical Theory of Evidence.* Princeton, NJ: Princeton University Press.

20. Zadeh, L. A., 1979. "A Theory of Approximate Reasoning." In *Machine Intelligence 9.* New York: John Wiley & Sons.

21. Zadeh, L. A., 1983. Lecture on Fuzzy Logic at George Washington University, Washington, DC, October 27.

22. Shortliffe, E. H., 1976. *Computer-Based Medical Consultations: MYCIN.* New York: American Elsevier.

23. Zadeh, L. A., 1983. "The Role of Fuzzy Logic in the Management of Uncertainty in Expert Systems." In *Fuzzy Sets and Systems.* Amsterdam: North-Holland.

24. Feigenbaum, E. A., 1982. "Applications-Oriented Artificial Intelligence Research: Medicine." In *Handbook of Artificial Intelligence, 2.* Los Altos, CA: HeurisTech Press.

25. Pfarr, T., 1983. Discussions at Computer Sciences Corporation, Silver Spring, MD.

26. Software A&E, 1983. *Knowledge Engineering System: Knowledge Base Author's Reference Manual.* Arlington, VA: Software Architecture & Engineering, Inc.

27. Software A&E, 1984. *KES: Knowledge Base Author's Reference Manual.* Arlington, VA: Software Architecture & Engineering, Inc.

28. Reggia, J. A., and Perricone, B. T., 1982. *KMS Manual.* College Park, MD: University of Maryland.

29. Software A&E, 1983. *Knowledge Engineering System: General Description Manual.* Arlington, VA: Software Architecture & Engineering, Inc.

30. Chorafas, D. N., 1987. *Applying Expert Systems in Business.* New York: McGraw-Hill, Inc.

31. Mishkoff, H. C., 1985. *Understanding Artificial Intelligence.* Dallas: Texas Instruments.

32. Bobrow, D. G., and Stefik, M. J., 1986. "Perspectives on Artificial Intelligence Programming." *Science,* 231, February 28.

33. Steele, G. L., 1984. *COMMON LISP.* Hudson, MA: Digital Press.

34. Clocksin, W. F., and Mellish, C. S., 1984. *Programming in PROLOG.* New York: Springer-Verlag.

35. Winston, P. H., and Horn, B. K. P., 1981. *LISP.* Reading, MA: Addison-Wesley.

36. Barber, G. R., 1987. "LISP vs. C for Implementing Expert Systems." *AI Expert,* 2, No. 2, February.

6 Expert System Shells

To help construct an expert system, an expert system shell could be used as a tool. It is the dialog structure and inference engine which, when linked to a knowledge base, functions as a fully operational expert system. An expert system shell can be useful for many reasons. One reason is that it can be a great time-saver in the expert system development process. With expert system shells the knowledge engineer doesn't have to reinvent the wheel and build an expert system from scratch, which could take 10 to 20 person-years to build. Instead, the knowledge engineer can concentrate on the development of the knowledge base, which is where the expert system derives its power, instead of concentrating on the dialog structure and the inference engine.

An expert system shell can also be helpful for prototyping purposes. With the use of a shell, an expert system prototype can be fairly quickly built (from 3 person-months to 1 person-year) to convince management that a full-scale expert system building effort is warranted.

A third benefit of using an expert system shell is that, if the expert system prototyping effort fails, not such a vast sum of resources would have been wasted as if the knowledge engineer would have constructed all of the expert system prototype from scratch.

The knowledge engineer, however, should beware of the adage: "For every task, there is a perfect shell." This is a false assumption, even though its converse is true. The knowledge engineer must recognize if a shell is appropriate for a particular task. In making this decision, several criteria could be used. This chapter will discuss these criteria, using examples from KES, EMYCIN, and ROSIE.

Criteria in Selecting Expert System Shells

Waterman and Hayes-Roth [1, 2] present criteria for evaluating expert system shells. These criteria, coupled with those from Liebowitz [3], are presented and categorized below:

USER-FRIENDLINESS

- High-level representation language for expressing procedural knowledge.
- Use of free-text comments.

- Good, accessible, and credible documentation.
- Built-in explanation and interaction facilities.

SHELL-EFFICIENCY

- Valid module for handling uncertainty.
- Parser capability.
- Local operating system accessibility.
- Basic general data representation scheme (database structure).
- Accessible control mechanism.

KNOWLEDGE ENGINEER-ORIENTED

- Knowledge engineer's access to shell.
- Cost of shell.
- Maintenance by shell developer.

HARDWARE-ORIENTED

- Necessary hardware configuration.
- Portability.

PROBLEM-ORIENTED

- Adaptability to current management approach.
- Appropriateness for problem considered.

User-Friendliness Criteria

Any user who has struggled with any system that was not developed with user-friendliness in mind can appreciate the benefit of having an expert system shell that truly assists the knowledge engineer with his task. Several aspects of user-friendliness will be considered here.

High-Level Representation Language

An expert system shell should provide a high-level representation language for expressing procedural knowledge [1]. Without such a language, the development process is slowed down and the system cannot be easily extended by the users. The language should be both readable and manageable by the knowledge engineers. For KES' production rule system, the representation language is KES.PS, which is then parsed into LISP-processable objects. An example of a rule in KES.PS is this:

```
rule1  if nature of mission=commandable,
       & satellite=pointer spacecraft,
       then characteristics=needed <0.8>.
```

EMYCIN [4] is comparable to KES in terms of a high-level representation language because rules can be entered in Abbreviated Rule Language, which is more English-like than LISP and can be modified with a high-level knowledge base editor [2]. Here is an example of an EMYCIN rule [1]:

```
If:    (1) The spilled substance is HF
Then:  It is definite (1.0) that the following is one
       of the recommended emergency procedures:
       Since the spill substance is HF--do not
       breathe it!
```

ROSIE [5] also has a high-level English-like representation language as do KES and EMYCIN, but it seems to lack structure in its rule format, as shown in the following [1]:

```
Before asserting chemical is HF:
Send  "Warning--do not breathe the spill material!",
      return.
End.
```

Most shells have a high-level English-like representation language that makes it easier for the knowledge engineer to implement the knowledge base.

Use of Free-Text Comments

Sometimes it is helpful, for easy understanding on the part of the user, to be able to supply free-text comments next to questions, rules, or answers supplied by the shell or user. KES and EMYCIN, for example, are capable of handling free-text comments. The attachments section in KES allows the use of free-text comments in such forms as explanations, questions, definitions, and rule rationale, as shown in previously mentioned Figure 5-7.

Good, Accessible, and Credible Documentation

From the point of view of the knowledge engineer, if documentation on the shell is not well-written, credible, and available, then learning how to use the shell will be extremely difficult.

Built-In Explanation and Interaction Facilities

Built-in explanation and interaction facilities speed prototype system development and facilitate initial testing and evaluation [1, 6]. An expert system should be able to explain its reasoning process in an understandable manner, which is an advantage over conventional computer programs. KES, for example, has the facility for free-text comments and various commands—such as explain, justify, and display—which add to explanation and interaction capabilities. The explanation capability in KES is facilitated by the *justify* command. In a labor issue eligibility expert system [7] implemented in KES, the following justification appears:

```
for eligible on labor issue=
  Claimant is not eligible for benefits based on the
  labor issues...
reasons for this statement:
  Labor dispute in progress during the week
  claimed=present
  Claimant and employer agree that a lockout is=
  absent
  Was claimant last employed by employer involved in
  the labor dispute=
  yes
  Participating or interested=
  yes
  (by rule: en1)
```

EMYCIN allows the user to enter keywords like WHY and HOW, and has a keyword parser that can interpret simple requests given in English [2]. By answering HOW in an EMYCIN-expert system for detecting bacterial infections in the blood, the following explanation resulted [2]:

```
HOW DID YOU DECIDE THAT ORGANISM-1 MIGHT BE AN E. COLI?
  I used RULE021 to conclude that the identity of
  ORGANISM-1 is e. coli.  This gave a cumulative CF
  of (.47).
  Then I used RULE084 to conclude that the identity
  of ORGANISM-1 is e. coli.  This gave a cumulative
  CF of (.55).
  Finally, I used RULE003 to conclude that the
  identity of ORGANISM-1 is e. coli.  This gave a
  cumulative CF of (.74).
```

This explanation is derived partly by the backward chaining of rules that takes place in EMYCIN.

Shell-Efficiency Criteria

Several factors govern the efficiency of an expert system shell. Five of these will be considered here.

Valid Module for Handling Uncertainty

Uncertainty needs to be expressed in an expert system due to such reasons as unavailable data, imperfect data, or omitted data. KES and EMYCIN have very well-tested ways of handling uncertainty and, under KES, uncertainty can be handled by an assortment of methods—certainty factors or Bayesian statistics—depending on which KES sub-system is used for the task. EMYCIN uses MYCIN's way of handling uncertainty (via certainty factors).

▌ Parser Capability

A **parsing** capability is a helpful feature in knowledge representation and programming. By having a parser, free-format English can be used, which would then be parsed into keywords and phrases for production rule development. KES, EMYCIN, and ROSIE have parsing facilities that are fairly sophisticated. The KES parser is invoked to transform a text file into an internally encoded knowledge base [8]. Any errors found during the parsing process will be flagged by the parser. The source text must then be modified using the text editor before submitting it to parsing again. EMYCIN and ROSIE have comparable parsing capabilities in which English-like language (used in the rules) is converted into LISP-processable objects.

▌ Local Operating System Accessibility

Accessing the local operating system provides greater flexibility in the shell as other languages or computer installations can be used. KES' ability to access the local operating system is through an external facility (*exit*). ROSIE, for example, has an interrupt mechanism, similar to KES', to handle new data upon arrival.

▌ Basic General Data Representation Scheme

The basic general data representation scheme relates to the database structure of the shell. This relates to the way the shell permits or encourages static knowledge to be represented. If it is too restrictive, even simple problems will be unsolvable; if it provides too much freedom, complex problems will seem overly complex [1]. The basic data representation scheme should be made as general as possible while keeping the representation task reasonably easy (i.e., constrained) for the target problems. By doing so, future changes in the knowledge base could be readily accommodated. ROSIE, for example, has no easy way to add or modify its own rules and no way to change its control structures to fit new problem domains [1].

▌ Accessible Control Mechanism

The form of the control shapes and restricts the representation of procedural knowledge in the system [1]. For example, the use of iteration, recursion, backward chaining, forward chaining, and hierarchies affects the choices for representing procedural knowledge. KES has three inference or control mechanisms that could be used (namely, rule-based, description-based, and Bayesian-based). EMYCIN has a relatively constrained and rigid control structure [1].

Knowledge Engineer-Oriented Criteria

Some of the factors governing the suitability of an expert system shell for a given task relate directly to the knowledge engineer and to the funds and assistance available to her/him.

▮ Knowledge Engineer's Access to the Shell

The knowledge engineer must have access to the necessary hardware needed to operate the shell. Some of the shells run only on LISP machines, where both the shell and the machine are very costly. Other shells run on the VAX computers, Apollos, microcomputers, and other hardware that may be readily available to the knowledge engineer.

▮ Cost of Shell

Expert system shells range from $49 to $6,500 on the microcomputers, and from about $24,000 to $72,000 on large machines. Shells could be very costly, and that is why it is important that the problem or task be carefully studied to see whether a shell is appropriate or not.

▮ Maintenance of Shell Developer

The shell should be currently maintained by the developer. An old tool, no longer supported by the developer, may be difficult to get running initially and could have basic system bugs that must be corrected by the user [1]. Most shell developers offer from one day to two weeks of training on how to operate the shell. Also, most shell developers will provide three days to a week of knowledge engineering consulting on-site where the expert system is being developed, to help in getting the "first" expert system developed.

Hardware-Oriented Criteria

At least two factors that must be considered when selecting an expert system shell relate directly to the hardware involved.

▮ Necessary Hardware Configuration

The configuration of the computer equipment that operates the shell is a major constraining factor in the suitability of the shell. KES, for example, runs on the VAX, CDC, UNIVAC, Apollo, Symbolics, and IBM PC/XT. EMYCIN operates principally on DEC mainframes. Again, shell selection must keep in mind the kind of hardware needed to run it.

▮ Portability

Portability, in this case, refers to using the shell on different computer hardware. KES has been converted, for example, from running on minicomputers to operating on microcomputers. Also, many shells are being converted from LISP-oriented languages to C and Ada programming languages. The ability to access these languages, for some tasks, is also an important consideration.

Problem-Oriented Criteria

No expert system shell should be chosen apart from serious consideration of the problem to be solved.

Adaptability to Current Management Approach

An expert system shell should be applicable to the current management approach and goals of the organization. For example, within NASA, there is a push for office automation and tools for helping managers make more effective decisions. Part of this office automation program involves an increasing number and use of microcomputers. Thus having an expert system shell that can run on the microcomputer might fit in nicely with the office automation plans.

Appropriateness for Problem Considered

This involves studying and analyzing the problem domain and task characteristics and then seeing which shells are able to handle these characteristics. For example, the problem domain characteristics for the command management system environment for READ involved a small to medium search space, predominantly categorical data, and uncertain knowledge. This means that the shell should at least have (1) search techniques to handle a small/medium search space, (2) a capability for handling production rules, and (3) modules to handle uncertainty, explanation, and interaction. Again, shells are *not* appropriate for all tasks. A task must be adequately studied before the examination of applicable shells can be accomplished.

Another Categorization of Criteria for Selecting an Expert System Shell

Forman and Nagy [9] have developed another set of criteria for selecting expert system shells. Their decomposition of criteria is shown below:

    I. COST

        A.   Acquisition cost

            1. Hardware cost: the cost of the hardware required to use the expert system shell.

            2. Software cost: the cost of the expert system shell itself.

            3. Operating systems: the cost of the operating systems and text editors and any additional software required to use the shell.

        B.   Development cost: the costs associated with the building, as distinct from the operation, of the expert system.

        C.   Operation cost: the cost associated with the routine use of the expert system.

II. THE PERSPECTIVE OF THE BUILDER/MAINTAINER OF THE EXPERT SYSTEM
   A. Learning: the ease of learning to use the expert system shell.
   B. Fuzzy: the ability to attach a certainty factor to the consequents of rules to indicate the level of certainty if the antecedent(s) of a rule were satisfied with complete confidence.
   C. Override: the ability to overrule the normal operation of the inference engine.
   D. Response: response time of the expert system shell to the commands of the builder or knowledge engineer.
   E. Maintenance: the relative ease of correcting problems in the knowledge base.
   F. Problem size: the largest problem that the expert system shell can handle, measured in number of rules.
   G. Exits and externals: the ease of leaving the expert system and passing values to and from alien code, including a database management system.

III. THE END USER'S PERSPECTIVE
   A. Fuzzy: the ability to hedge responses to questions from the expert system by indicating level of belief in the response given.
   B. What-if: the ease of assessing the impact of changing responses to questions.
   C. Modes of input: the ease of inputing responses to the expert system from tape or disk files rather than from the keyboard.
   D. Justification: explanation of final and intermediate conclusions reached and explanation for questions posed to the end user.
   E. Dialogue: the quality of the questions from the expert system and of responses to end-user commands.
   F. Response: the response time of the expert system during the end-user consultation.

IV. EXPERT SYSTEM SHELL'S VENDOR
   A. Training: initial help offered to customers.
   B. Hot line: emergency service offered to customers.
   C. Consulting: consultation service offered to customers.
   D. Portability of the expert system shell: number of different types of processors that the shell runs on and the ease of converting the shell to run on additional types of processors.
   E. Viability: long-term prospects of the vendor (will the vendor be around in a few years if we need something?).

This set of criteria overlaps the first set presented. Nonetheless, the knowledge engineer should take both sets of criteria into consideration when deciding between expert system shells.

Examples of Expert System Shells

About 30 to 40 expert system shells have been developed to aid in the expert system building process. Shells have been designed for both the "large machines" (i.e., minicomputers and mainframes) and the microcomputers, as well as the specialized LISP machines. For the large machines the expert system shells ART [10], KEE [11], Knowledge Craft [12], S.1 [13], KES [14], and TIMM [15] have been used quite extensively. They typically have multiple ways of representing knowledge and search strategies, and usually have helpful debugging tools for knowledge base refinement. The prices, as of May 1987, for these shells range from $24,000 to $72,000, depending on the capabilities of the shell. These prices, however, will be decreasing over the coming years as competition will force the prices down. Other examples of expert system shells for large machines are shown here:

RULE-BASED AND FRAME-BASED:

ADVISE	University of Illinois
PICON	Lisp Machines, Inc.
GEN-X	General Electric
LES	Lockheed
PLUME	Carnegie Group

RULE-BASED:

EMYCIN	Stanford University
EXPERT	Rutgers University
ROSIE	Rand Corporation
AGE	Stanford University
GPSI	University of Illinois
HEARSAY-III	U.S.C./Information Sciences Institute
KAS	SRI
PRISM	IBM
SAVOIR	ISI (United Kingdom)
ARBY	Smart Systems
TEIRESIAS	Stanford University
RULEMASTER	Radian Corporation
REVEAL	Infotym

Besides the expert system shells for the large machines, expert system shells have been developed for the microcomputers. Their prices, as of May 1987, vary from $49 to $6,500, depending on the shell's capabilities. Examples of expert system shells that run on the microcomputer are listed here:

RULE-BASED:

M.1	Teknowledge, Inc.
Personal Consultant/ Personal Consultant Plus	Texas Instruments, Inc.
SeRIS	SRI
ACLS	Intelligent Terminals Ltd.
ES/P Advisor	Expert Systems Int.
INSIGHT/INSIGHT 2	Level 5 Corporation
AL/X	University of Edinburgh

Exsys	Exsys, Inc.
Guru	Micro Database Systems
Xsys	California Intelligence
Reveal	Infotym
TIMM-PC	General Research Corp.
Rulemaster	Radian Corporation
KES	Software Architecture & Engineering
GoldWorks	Gold Hill Computers
VP-Expert	Paperback Software
Micro-Expert	McGraw-Hill
1st-Class	Programs in Motion, Inc.

EXAMPLE-BASED:

Expert-Ease/Expert-Edge	Human Edge Software
K:Base	Gold Hill Computers
KDS	Knowledge Development Systems

If the knowledge engineer wants to use the microcomputer and if these microcomputer-based expert system shells are not adequate to fit the task's characteristics, an assortment of LISP and PROLOG programming languages might be used. For the microcomputer, various LISP and PROLOG dialects are shown here:

BYSO LISP	Levien Instrument Co.
Golden Common LISP	Gold Hill Computers
IQLISP	Integral Quality, Inc.
LISP/88	Norell Data Systems
Micro-PROLOG	Programming Logic Systems, Inc.
MULISP/83	Microsoft Corp.
PROLOG-1	Expert Systems Int.
PROLOG-86	Solution Systems
Turbo Prolog	Borland
TLC LISP	The LISP Company
XLISP	PC-SIG (public domain software)

TOPSI, by Dynamic Master Systems, is a rule-based programming language that could also be used on the microcomputer.

Various dialects of LISP and PROLOG also exist for the large machines, such as Inter LISP, Mac LISP, Franz LISP, and others. Besides these dialects, other programming languages are available for use on the large machines, as indicated:

RULE-BASED:

OPS 5	Digital Equipment Corporation
OPS 5e	Verac Corporation
OPS 83	Production Systems Technologies, Inc.
YAPS	University of Maryland

FRAME-BASED:

RLL	Stanford University
UNITS	Stanford University
FRL	MIT

LOGIC-BASED (LANGUAGES, LIKE PROLOG, BASED ON FIRST-ORDER PREDICATE CALCULUS):

DUCK	Smart Systems

OBJECT-ORIENTED (LANGUAGES THAT MANIPULATE OBJECTS USED FOR DECLARATIVE KNOWLEDGE):

LOOPS	Xerox PARC
Smalltalk-80	Tektronix/Xerox PARC
(Smalltalk/V for the PC)	Digitalk, Inc.

By using the criteria previously discussed in this chapter, the selection of an expert system shell or programming language, if appropriate, will be made much easier.

References

1. Waterman, D. A., and Hayes-Roth, F., 1982. *An Investigation of Tools for Building Expert Systems.* Santa Monica, CA: Rand Corporation.

2. Hayes-Roth, F., Waterman, D. A., and Lenat, D. B., 1983. *Building Expert Systems.* Reading, MA: Addison-Wesley.

3. Liebowitz, J., 1985. *Determining Functional Requirements For NASA Goddard's Command Management System Software Design Using Expert Systems.* D.Sc. dissertation, George Washington University, Washington, DC.

4. van Melle, W., Shortliffe, E. H., and Buchanan, B. G., 1984. "EMYCIN: A Knowledge Engineer's Tool for Contructing Rule-Based Expert Systems." In *Rule-Based Expert Systems: The MYCIN Experiments of the Stanford Heuristic Programming Project*, eds. B. G. Buchanan and E. H. Shortliffe. Reading, MA: Addison-Wesley.

5. Fain, J., Gorlin, D., Hayes-Roth, F., Rosenschein, S., Sowizral, H., and Waterman, D., 1981. *The ROSIE Language Reference Manual.* Rand Note N–1647–ARPA. Santa Monica, CA: Rand Corporation.

6. Shoeben, A. M., 1981. *Expert Systems: Newest Brainchild of Computer Science.* Rand Corporation Report. Santa Monica, CA: Rand Corporation.

7. Nagy, T. J., DiSciullo, J., and Crosslin, R., 1983. "Reducing Costs and Improving Services in Unemployment Insurance Nonmonetary Determinations Using Expert Systems." *U.I. Research Exchange,* Fall.

8. Software A&E, 1983. *Knowledge Engineering System: Knowledge Base Author's Reference Manual.* Arlington, VA: Software Architecture & Engineering, Inc.

9. Forman, E. H., and Nagy, T. J., 1985. "A Multicriteria Model to Select An Expert System Generator." In *Proceedings of the Expert Systems in Government Conference.* Washington, DC: IEEE/MITRE.

10. Clayton, B. D., 1984. *ART Programmer Primer.* Los Angeles, CA: Inference Corporation.

11. Kunz, J. C., Kehler, T. P., and Williams, M. D., 1984. "Applications Development Using a Hybrid AI Development System." *The AI Magazine*, 5, No. 3.

12. Carnegie Group, Inc., 1984. *Knowledge Craft Manual*. Pittsburgh, PA.

13. Teknowledge, Inc., 1984. *S.1 Product Description*. Palo Alto, CA.

14. Software A&E, 1984. *KES: Knowledge Base Author's Manual*. Arlington, VA: Software Architecture & Engineering, Inc.

15. Kiselewich, S., 1983. *TIMM—The Intelligent Machine Model*. Santa Barbara, CA: General Research Corporation.

7 Human Factors Considerations for Expert Systems

Human factors addresses the entire man/machine system, including all interfaces between man, machine, and the environment in which they are embedded [1]. It is recognized that these interactions between man and machine are critical factors in the success of automated systems [1, 2]. Having "good" human factors in the expert system design is vital for the success and use of the expert system. Sometimes, however, human factor considerations are omitted due to lack of time and money, lack of qualified human factors specialists, or lack of communication on interdisciplinary issues [3]. This chapter will address some of the human factors features that should be considered when building an expert system. These features have been incorporated into READ and will be shown throughout the chapter.

Human Factors Features in Expert Systems

Human factors engineering plays an important role in expert systems [4, 5]. In fact, a study performed in Europe [11] indicated that in a typical expert system, 8% of the code is the inference engine, 22% is the knowledge base, and *44% is involved in user input and output*. The study also indicated that with expert system prototypes, *70% of the effort went into developing the man/machine interface of the prototype* [11]. This attitude is also reflected by the authors of MYCIN [6], for example, as they even went to the following detail:

1. Developing user aids that were available at any time through the use of HELP and question mark commands.

2.   Allowing the system automatically to correct spelling errors when it was 'obvious' what the user meant.

3.   Allowing the physician to enter only the first few characters of a response if what was entered uniquely defined the intended answer.

The human factors features that should be considered when building an expert system are the use of messages, menus, precautions against undesirable input, free-text attachments, help function, and justification facility. Each of these features will be discussed in turn.

▌ Messages

One of the human factors design considerations that should be incorporated into an expert system is the use of messages. Constructive and helpful messages could be used to do several things:

1.   Provide instructions for operating the expert system.

2.   Provide reasons if being exited from the expert system.

3.   Provide descriptions of some pertinent commands and how to use them.

4.   Acknowledge the end of the user session, and provide information for restarting or ending the user–expert system session.

5.   Allow for information rephrase.

6.   Put conclusions into perspective.

Examples of some of these messages, taken from a user session of READ, are shown below:

> These are the major characteristics influencing CMS software functional requirements determination for a new satellite. Each characteristic will now be displayed along with its associated value(s) and certainty factor(s). The certainty factor ranges inclusively from -1.0 (absolutely false) to 1.0 (absolutely true), and its default value is 1.0.
>
> .
>
> .
>
> .
>
> coupling and interrelationships between experiments:
>   present <1.0>

Messages guide the user through the expert system session and they keep the user informed as to what is happening during the session. A pause command might be used in the expert system to allow time for the user to read the instructions for operating the expert system [7]. In addition to the pause command, the phrase "ready for command" could be used instead of the imperative form "enter command." "Ready for command" gives the user a feeling that he/she is in control of the expert system, instead of creating an inferiority feeling that the computer is in control of the user.

▌ Menus

A second technique used in an expert system for effective end-user interface design is the use of menus. Menus allow the user to choose what he/she would like the expert system to perform. Menus allow users simply to recognize items rather than to recall them [8]. To prevent menus from becoming tedious if the choices are too finely detailed [9], the expert system should be able to handle "unknown" or "none" if the user is not sure of the answer or feels none of the answers applies. Menus may be used in the expert system to do several things:

1. Determine if the user wants to begin the session.
2. Determine if the user would like references displayed.
3. Ask the user if he/she wants
   a. to obtain a justification of the results just reached by the expert system.
   b. to continue to obtain more detailed results.
   c. to determine the results for another case.
   d. to stop.

An example of a menu used in READ is shown through an excerpt of a user session:

```
What do you want to do now


(1) get a justification of the first level requirements
reached by READ
(2) continue to obtain the second and third level
requirements
(3) determine requirements for another satellite
(4) stop--I am finished
= ? (multiple answers permitted)  2


user needs for certain observations:


(1) absent
(2) present
= ? explain
            .

            .

            .
```

Appendix B shows other menus used in READ.

The previous menu is referenced in the actions section of READ's knowledge base as follows:

```
askfor menu.
if menu = justification
then
message  "If you would like further amplification of the"
         "justification simply type 'display rationale"
         "(rule name)' where"
```

```
             "rule name is the one indicated below.  To"
             "display the rule itself, type 'display (rule"
             "name)'."
             " "
             "The following are the justifications for the"
             "first level requirements that were reached:",
     justify level one functional requirements,
     obtain level two functional requirements.
     if menu = advance
     then
     obtain level two functional requirements.
     if menu = another
     then next case.
     if menu = halt
     then stop.
```

Precautions Against Undesirable Input

The third human factors design that might be useful in an expert system is to include precautions against undesirable inputs [7]. For example, extra rules were incorporated into the rule section of READ's knowledge base to defend against incongruent input, as shown by the following rule:

```
rule2  if nature of mission = commandable,
       & nature of mission = not commandable,
       then characteristics = none,
       message "A mission cannot be both
         commandable and not commandable",
        stop.
```

This rule prevents the user from answering that a satellite is both commandable and not commandable. The human factors could be improved in this rule because there isn't any constructive message saying that the user is being exited from the system and how the user can restart the session. Rules were also used in the actions section of READ to prevent the generation of lower-level requirements if the answers for the higher-level requirements were all unknown (see Figure 5-8).

Attachments

Another human factors design element is to use attachments in the knowledge base [7]. Attachments allow for free-text comments and they can be used, as shown in Figures 4-3 and 5-7 and Appendix B, as follows:

1.   To provide descriptions of attributes and attribute values (*explain* attachment).

2.   To allow for system-generated questions to be posed to the user (*question* attachment).

3.   To allow for synonyms of attributes to be used when typing the knowledge base (*synonyms* attachment).

4.   To provide rationale for rules (*rationale* attachment).

Through the use of these attachments, the user could obtain descriptions and definitions of attributes, attribute values, and rules if the user were unsure of the meaning of particular items. For example, an excerpt of a sample user session of READ is shown:

```
command sequencing planning aids:

(1) absent
(2) present
  ?  2


instrument management aids:

(1) absent
(2) present
  ?  2


initial orbit:

(1) complex
(2) average
(3) simple
  ? explain 1


Command encountered--deferring current question

Refers to very complex and protracted initial
stabilization and attitude control.

Continuing previous line of questioning

initial orbit:

(1) complex
(2) average
(3) simple
  ? explain 3


Command encountered--deferring current question

Refers to very little or no special software or
support required for initial stabilization and control.

Continuing previous line of questioning
```

```
initial orbit:

(1) complex
(2) average
(3) simple
  ?  1

spacecraft subsystem contingencies:

(1) complex--very complex recovery planned
(2) average--complex recovery planned
(3) simple--simple recovery procedures
  ?  1

special viewing periods:

(1) complex--major enhancement of normal CMS
(2) average--special software needed
(3) simple--little special software needed
  ?  1

simulator:

(1) absent
(2) present
  ?  2

user independence:

(1) complex--high independence
(2) average--medium independence
(3) simple--low independence
  ?  explain

Command encountered--deferring current question

Refers to the flexibility of the experimenter in
command and control activities.

Continuing previous line of questioning

user independence:

(1) complex--high independence
(2) average--medium independence
(3) simple--low independence
  ?  1
```

```
data security:

(1) complex--highly proprietary data
(2) average--medium proprietary data
(3) simple--low proprietary data
  ?  1
     .
     .
     .
```

In this example the user did not understand what "complex" and "simple" meant for initial orbit. The user typed "explain 1" and "explain 3," respectively, to obtain descriptions, via the explain attachment, for the attribute values "complex" and "simple." The explain attachment is developed by the knowledge engineer, and is included in the attributes section of READ's knowledge base. Also shown in this sample dialog, the user typed "explain" to get a description for "user independence." KES has very good human factors design because, in the case of typing "explain" for "user independence," messages are printed before and after the description to keep the user informed of what is happening during the session. As shown in the user session, the message "Command encountered— deferring current question" is printed before the description of "user independence," whereafter the message "Continuing previous line of reasoning" is printed. The question is then reasked to the user so the user can put the chosen value of "user independence." If there were not a description for "user independence," then READ would respond, "No explanation available."

❙ Help Function

Another facility for improving the user/computer interface is having a *help* function. If the user doesn't know what command to use or wants a description of a command, the help function could be useful in providing a list of commands and their descriptions. If the user responds by typing "help" to a question, KES would generate the following message:

```
= ?  (multiple answers permitted)  help

Command encountered--deferring current question

Try 'help answer' or 'help command'
you may also type 'help <command>' where <command> is
any valid KES command.

Note:  in all command descriptions; angular brackets
('<,>') indicate that you substitute a valid
attribute, value, or rule name, as appropriate, for
the enclosed word.  Do not type the brackets.

ready for command:
     .
     .
     .
```

One of the axioms for ease of use is: "Help systems are necessary" [9]. With the "help" function, the user can obtain additional guidance in operating the expert system.

Besides help functions, the paging of text should be well organized if screens are being used [7]. The monitor should not be so full of information that it becomes cluttered. Also, when developing the value sets of attributes, minimize the number of answers needed for a question. If too many answers are presented to the user (i.e., over seven items), this places a limitation on the user's short-term memory.

▌ Justification Facility

Separate attention should be given to a justification facility in an expert system. Some researchers believe a capability for justification is one of the most important features that an expert system can have [10]. It reassures a human observer of the validity of a chain of inference steps. In the MYCIN experiments the program provides a justification for the therapy selection, which includes the reasons for selecting one antimicrobial instead of another [6]. Also available in MYCIN is an explanation of the calculations used to decide on a dose. Likewise, in KES, a justification facility is provided so that conclusions can be justified in the following form:

```
a=b
reasons for this statement:

c=d
.
.
.
f=g
(by rule: x1)
```

An excerpt from a user session of READ, where the justification process was invoked for level two functional requirements, is shown next. This shows a partial listing of the "justified" level two requirements:

```
for level two functional requirements=
   model reaction wheel speeds...

Reasons for this statement:
  level one functional requirements=
   mission scheduling and planning
  need for wheel speeds=
   present
  (by rule:  rule46 <1.0>)

for level two functional requirements=
   predict system power usage...
```

```
Reasons for this statement:
  level one functional requirements=
   mission scheduling and planning
  safety considerations=
   present
  need for power profile report=
   present
  (by rule:  rule47 <1.0>)

for level two functional requirements=
  monitor system power usage...

Reasons for this statement:
  level one functional requirements=
   mission scheduling and planning
  (by rule:  rule48 <1.0>)

for level two functional requirements=
  generate composite maneuver parameters...

Reasons for this statement:
  level one functional requirements=
   mission scheduling and planning
  (by rule:  rule48 <1.0>)

for level two functional requirements=
  adjust scheduled time...

Reasons for this statement:
  level one functional requirements=
   mission scheduling and planning
  safety considerations=
   present
  need for constraint checking function=
   present
  (by rule:  rule49 <1.0>)

for level two functional requirements=
  translate stored command processor command results...

Reasons for this statement:
  circum=
   need to translate command requests
  (by rule:  rule53 <0.5>)
           .

           .

           .
```

The justification facility is vital because the user can see how and why certain attribute values were determined, which creates trust and believability regarding the expert system. For example, as shown in the previous listing, "model reaction wheel speeds" was determined as a second-level requirement because, by rule46:

```
        level one functional requirements=
            mission scheduling and planning
    AND   the need for wheel speeds=present.
```

To provide more information in this justification process, the user could type in, while using READ, "display rationale (rule name)" to get a description of a rule based on the free-text "rationale" attachment designed by the knowledge engineer in the rule section of the knowledge base. For example:

```
=  ?  display rationale (rule76)


Command encountered--deferring current question


This is needed to know if packetization is present.


Continuing previous line of questioning
```

Also, the user could type "display (rule name)" to obtain the contents of a specific rule.
Human factors features are critical to the success of an expert system. If an expert system is difficult to use, even though it is reliable, this creates an implementation barrier. An expert system is not just a collection of rules. It must have the proper human factors features to make it accessible and useful.

References

1. Simes, D. K., and Sirsky, P. A., 1983. *Analytic Tools for Human Factors: The Psychology of Man-Machine Dialogues*. Washington, DC: Air Force Data Services Center.
2. Shneiderman, B., 1982. "System Message Design: Guidelines and Experimental Results." In *Directions in Human/Computer Interaction*, eds. A. Badre and B. Shneiderman . Norwood, NJ: Ablex Publishing.
3. Simes, D. K., and Sirsky, P. A., 1983. *Human Factors: An Exploration of the Psychology of Man-Machine Dialogues*. Washington, DC: Air Force Data Services Center.
4. Reitman, W., 1984. *Artificial Intelligence Applications For Business*. Norwood, NJ: Ablex Publishing.
5. Michaelis, P. R., Miller, M. L., and Hendler, J. A., 1982. "Artificial Intelligence and Human Factors Engineering: A Necessary Synergism in the Interface of the Future." In *Directions in Human/Computer Interaction*, eds. A. Badre and B. Shneiderman. Norwood, NJ: Ablex Publishing.
6. Buchanan, B., and Shortliffe, E. H., 1984. *Rule-Based Expert Systems: The MYCIN Experiments of the Stanford Heuristic Programming Project*. Reading, MA: Addison-Wesley.
7. Software A&E, 1984. *Knowledge Engineering System: Knowledge Base Author's Reference Manual*. Arlington, VA: Software Architecture & Engineering, Inc.
8. Allen, R. B., 1982. "Cognitive Factors in Human Interaction with Computers." In *Directions in Human/Computer Interaction*, eds. A. Badre and B. Shneiderman. Norwood, NJ: Ablex Publishing.

9. Savage, R. E., and Habinek, J. K., 1984. "A Multilevel Menu-Driven User Interface: Design and Evaluation Through Simulation." In *Human Factors in Computer Systems*, eds. J. C. Thomas and M. L. Schneider. Norwood, NJ: Ablex Publishing.

10. Hayes-Roth, F., Waterman, D. A., and Lenat, D. B., 1983. *Building Expert Systems*. Reading, MA: Addison-Wesley.

11. Berry, D. C., and Broadbent, D. E., 1987. "Expert Systems and the Man-Machine Interface—Part Two: The User Interface." *Expert Systems*, 4, No. 1.

8 Knowledge Validation

After performing the knowledge programming step, the next stage in the expert system life cycle is knowledge validation. Validation is an essential phase in a software product's life cycle. Buchanan et al. [1] stress that validation of the rules that organize knowledge should be accomplished in the knowledge acquisition process of an expert system. Validation could influence refinements on the formulation of the rules (implementation stage) and on the design structure that organizes the knowledge (formalization stage), and reformulations on the knowledge representation concepts (conceptualization stage) and problem characteristics identification (identification stage) [1]. Validation is the means for determining the accuracy of the software, which influences if the software performs the way it was promised (by the software designers) to be performed. With expert systems one is trying to test the quality of the system's decisions and advice, and the correctness of the reasoning techniques. Testing and validation is an iterative task that is performed during the expert system development cycle. Through testing and validation, knowledge refinement can be made to correct such common errors as omitted rules, incorrect rules, incorrect association of rules, special cases overlooked, and omitted useful relationships. This chapter will discuss some validation approaches that could be used, as well as explain some validation results from READ.

Validation Approaches

Several techniques are available for the validation of software. One such technique refers to static analysis. Static analysis usually does not involve the actual execution of code. According to Adrion et al. [2], most static analysis is performed by parsers and associated translators residing in compilers. The parser detects errors ranging in complexity from ill-formed arithmetic expressions to complex type-incompatibilities. KES, for example, provides two tools that help in static analysis—the Parser and Inspector. The KES Parser detects a wide variety of syntax errors and inconsistencies [3]. Two common syntax errors are "missing delimiter" (for example, a missing comma or parenthesis), and "attribute name is undefined or has no value." Inspector, contained in the production rule subsystem of KES (KES.PS), provides a number of capabilities to aid in static analysis, including detection of unattached attributes (i.e., attributes with undeclared values) and direct/ indirect recursions (i.e., operations that are defined in terms of themselves), and derivation of the actual attribute hierarchy from the knowledge base.

Besides static analysis, another validation approach deals with error rate. This, the most widely used method of validation [4], involves counting the number of correct or incorrect classifications the expert system produces [3]. This method is quite appealing because of its ease of use, but there are two potential drawbacks [4]. First, the error rate is insensitive and thus doesn't take into account the magnitude of an error. Second, the use of error rates to assess predictions fails to distinguish a decision from the evidence on which that decision is based. In spite of these drawbacks, the error rate approach is still the most popular validation technique.

Proof of correctness is another common validation technique. These proofs can be formal or informal. Proof techniques consist of validating the consistency of an output assertion with respect to a program (or requirement specification) and an input assertion [2]. This technique is also used for verification of software.

A validation approach by Shapiro [4] uses a measure of predictive accuracy. This measure assesses the accuracy of the probabilities asserted, as opposed to scoring the all-or-none rectitude of decisions. The measure, denoted by Q, is

$$Q = \sum_{i=1}^{n} (\log_2 p_i^* + 1)/n,$$

where:

$$p_i^* = p_i \quad \text{if the event occurred in the } i\text{th case (estimated probability)}$$
$$p_i^* = 1-p_i \quad \text{if the event did not occur in the } i\text{th case}$$
$$n = \text{number of predictions}$$

This approach offers a graded means of validation in contrast to the right-or-wrong measure of factual knowledge used in more traditional validation methods [4].

Another approach to validation is the use of the Kappa statistic. The Kappa statistic, K, was proposed by Cohen [5] as a coefficient of agreement for nominal scales:

$$K = \frac{p_o - p_c}{1 - p_c}$$

where:

$$p_o = \text{observed proportion of agreement}$$
$$p_c = \text{proportion of agreement expected by chance}$$

Cohen has improved upon this concept by developing a weighted Kappa statistic, K_w, which is the proportion of *weighted* agreement corrected for chance. The use of unequal weights for symmetrical cells makes K_w suitable as a measure of validity (refer to Cohen [5] for further details).

Dynamic analysis techniques can also be used for validation. Dynamic analysis requires that the program be executed—that is, the program is run on some test cases and the results of the program's performance are examined to check whether the program operated as expected [2]. Some typical techniques are dynamic assertions [6], expression analysis, flow analysis, and timing analysis [2]. Simulation can also be used throughout the software development process to verify and validate that the specification and performance requirements are satisfied at every phase [7].

Another validation approach deals with backcasting, which involves running the model on a past case to see if the results from the model are the same as the historical results. One way to compare the test results with historical (or documented) results is through analogy. The works of Gentner [8] and Silverman [9] use analogy as a comparison methodology.

Their hybrid method is a coordinate system for analogical measurement [9]. The focus on this approach is on the mapping of objects and relations between objects [8]. Objects may be clear entities (e.g., "rabbit"), component parts of a larger object (e.g., "rabbit's ear"), or even coherent combinations of smaller units (e.g., "litter of rabbits"); the important point is that they function as wholes at a given level of organization. Relations express propositions about the objects and take on two or more arguments [8]. For example, collide (x, y) is a relation that expresses a collision between objects x and y. Once an analogy is given, it can be measured on ten dimensions [9]: specificity, clarity, richness, abstractness, systematicity, procedurality, contextuality, diagnosticity, temporality, and validity. By using this construct, the "goodness" of analogies can be measured.

The next section will discuss the validation of READ.

Case Study: Validation of READ

READ's validation involved the use of the KES Parser, Inspector, and backcasting. After numerous, successive tries of encoding the knowledge base and then activating KES.PS, a number of errors were identified by the parser. Most of these errors were related to undeclared attribute names, and a few errors related to missing delimiters (i.e., punctuation marks or "tokens"). To correct the errors relating to undeclared attributes, the missing attribute names were encoded into the attributes section of the knowledge base. Missing delimiters related primarily to punctuation errors, such as a missing parenthesis, comma, or period. The undeclared attributes and missing delimiter errors were easy to locate because when the user typed "@addlist (filename)", the knowledge base was printed and many of the errors appeared directly under the line in which they occurred.

Other inconsistencies appeared throughout the iterative development of the knowledge base. A common inconsistency was that the attribute type did not match the attribute. For example, "real time user response (mlt): absent, present." means that real-time user response is a multiple-type attribute whose values can be absent and/or present. An inconsistency exists because real-time user response can't be both absent and present; it can be only one or the other. In this case the attribute type should have been single (sgl) instead of a multiple type (mlt).

Besides using the parser for validation, Inspector was also used for validating the expert system and refining the knowledge. Inspector was particularly useful in uncovering direct/indirect recursions in the knowledge base. Direct and indirect recursion contained in the rules of a KES.PS knowledge base can cause its execution to enter a recursive loop. Inspector did locate indirect recursion in the expert system. This recursion related to Rule 1 (if pointer mission=present then scanner mission=absent) and Rule 2 (if scanner mission=present then pointer mission=absent). Here indirect recursion exists because the determination of pointer mission is based on scanner mission (Rule 2), but the determination of scanner mission is based on pointer mission (Rule 1). The recursion was corrected by deleting Rule 2 and leaving in Rule 1, as shown:

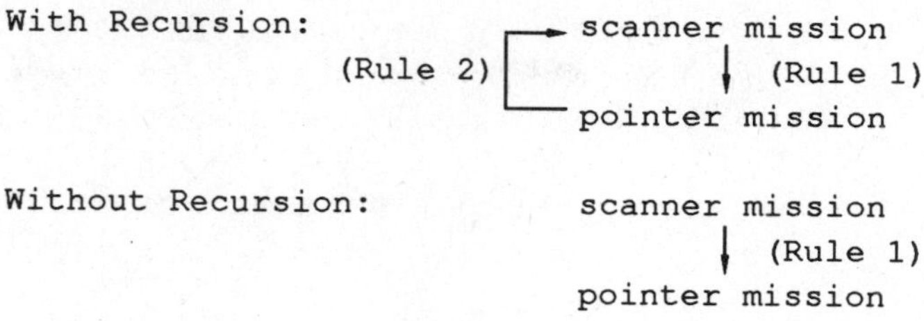

Besides using Inspector and the Parser, backcasting was used, in which test cases of previous satellites were run against the expert system to see if the expert system derived the same lists of command management system (CMS) requirements as those of the documented requirements for each of the satellites. Two major factors complicated this process. These relate to availability and contextuality.

Availability refers to the accessibility of information and the display of that information in a readily available form. Part of the difficulty in testing READ was that the documents containing a satellite's CMS software functional requirements were hard to locate. These documents had been written (e.g., Requirements Document, Preliminary Design Document, and Critical Design Review Document), but they hadn't been archived in a central location. Part of the problem was because NASA's "corporate memory" had not been adequately developed, which made it inaccessible for collecting and retrieving CMS documents. Without available documentation, a potential bias may result in which individuals involved in the knowledge acquisition process may opt for inferior and oftentimes mistaken, but more readily available, analogs [10].

Contextuality was the other main factor that increased the complexity of READ's testing. *Contextuality* refers to the degree to which language, physical forms, or knowledge pertaining to an alternative being considered for the base is specific to that alternative (i.e., the degree of standardization of the language used to describe the expert system-derived and documented requirements). In the CMS environment, contextuality involves the consistency of the language used to describe requirements in CMS documents from one satellite to another. This relates to the standardization of language in defining requirements; over the past ten years this has not been consistent or generic in nature. For example, the Solar Maximum Mission (SMM) satellite's level one functional requirement for "Command Loading" is called the "Load Generator Function." Table 8-1 shows the degree of mismatch/match between the wording of the documented requirements and that of READ's requirements for the test cases—Space Telescope (ST), Solar Maximum Mission satellite (SMM), and Dynamics Explorer satellite (DE). To account for this discrepancy of language to see whether the expert system-derived requirements matched the documented requirements, it was necessary to have a "translated or interpreted" version of requirements, which served to translate the language of the documented requirements into that of the expert system-derived requirements. This translation process was facilitated by reviewing various documentation for a satellite and, most importantly, having a NASA CMS specialist (who is knowledgeable about the CMS requirements for a specific satellite) interpret the documented set of requirements with the expert system's set. Analogical mapping, using Gentner's [8] and Silverman's [9] frameworks, was used to compare the translated requirements with the expert system's requirements. Liebowitz [10] goes into detail as to how this mapping was accomplished. Because of the difficulty in finding individuals (and documentation) who were able to develop the "translated" versions of requirements, only one function of a single satellite (i.e., the generator function of SMM) was translated.

Table 8-1

Degree of mismatch/match between the wording of the documented requirements and that of the expert system (E.S.) requirements[a]

Test Case			# of E.S.-Generated Reqs.	# of Doc. Reqs.	# of E.S. to Doc. Matches of Similar Wording	# of E.S. to Doc. Mismatches of Similar Wording	# of E.S. Reqs. that Should not Be Listed[a]	# of Doc. Reqs. that Were Omitted But Should not Have Been Omitted[b]
1. Model Case:								
ST	:	Level 1	6	6	6	0	0	0
		Level 2	36	36	36	0	0	0
		Level 3	139	139	139	0	0	0
2. SMM	:	Level 1	6	3	0	6	0	0
		Level 2	31	14	3	28	0	1
		Level 3	76	72	5	71	8	0
3. DE	:	Level 1	6	3	1	5	0	2
		Level 2	13	11	0	13	0	0
		Level 3	30	21	1	29	4	0

[a]Sources:

1. Computer Sciences Corporation, *Space Telescope POCC Applications Software Support Functional Requirements*, Contract NAS5–26685, July 1983.
2. Computer Sciences Corporation, *Command Management System for Solar Maximum Mission*, Critical Design Review, December 1978.
3. Computer Sciences Corporation, Updates to DE-A and -B Command Management System Requirement Definitions, Contract NAS5–24300, June 1980.

[b]4. Discussion with Thomas Pfarr, of Computer Sciences Corporation, and Patricia Lightfoot, Nancy Goodman, and Robert Dutilly, of NASA Goddard.

There were several problems with this validation process. One major limitation was that there was a large reliance on the validator's interpretation of the requirement comparisons and definitions. Also, there was a tendency for "force fitting" of matching documented requirements to expert system requirements to avoid redevelopment of the expert system. Additionally, a tremendous opportunity for bias is created when the validator of the expert system and the domain expert are the same individual, as in this case. Last, several validators and several test cases should have been used to validate READ. Taking into account these limitations, the translation process showed that for a single function of a single satellite, READ fared well even though the match-up (i.e., exact wording) failed between the documented requirements and READ's requirements.

Validation is an extremely important part of the knowledge engineering process. Many test cases are typically used to assess the accuracy of the expert system's performance. With R1/XCON, for example, it has taken over 80,000 orders to uncover some of the inadequacies in R1/XCON's configuration knowledge. It is not necessary to use as many test cases as in R1/XCON's example, but the accuracy of the expert system should be tested to the point where the expert system at least meets the acceptance rate (i.e., the percentage of the time that the expert system must be correct in its decisions) established by the client. In other words, there should be enough of a variety of test cases to ensure the quality and reasoning of the expert system's decisions, and to test the system to know the point where it degrades quickly.

Lessons to Be Learned from READ's Validation Experience

Several lessons were learned from the validation process of READ. These will hopefully benefit future knowledge engineers involved in the validation stage of an expert system:

- It is helpful to have readily available test cases when selecting a task for expert system application.
- Consistency and standardization of language should appear among the test cases.
- Many test cases and many validators should be used.
- Blind verification studies are helpful in testing the expert system. This means that the validators do not know if the results of a sample test case are from the expert system or a validator.
- Beware of potential bias on the part of the domain expert if he/she is being used as a validator.
- Prepare test cases that cover not only the "black and white" areas, but also the "gray" areas.
- Check not only the quality of the expert system's advice, but also the reasoning that it uses to arrive at the decision. The "correct" advice could be derived from the expert system through faulty reasoning. For example, an expert system might diagnose that an individual has a particular illness. However, the reasoning used to arrive at that conclusion might be found to be wrong when the user sees the explanations of the expert system's reasoning. It is the same thing as getting an answer from a computer program without any syntax errors, but knowing the answer is ludicrous due to possible logical errors in the program (i.e., garbage-in, garbage-out). Thus it is important to have some redundancy built into the expert system to act as a "double-check" on the expert system's reasoning when a combination of rules is employed. Special test cases of events which occur infrequently might also weed out pollution in the knowledge base.

- Beware of implementation barriers. Potential barriers and possible solutions include the following:

   Learning to use the expert system
   —have training sessions
   —write good documentation

   Animosities by experts in using the expert system
   —work closely with experts
   —incorporate comments and feedback
   —perform backcasting and testing

   Why change?
   —make their job easier

   Users may disagree on expert system results
   —employ certainty factors or way for handling uncertainty
   —perform proper validation and testing

   Users feel the expert system doesn't represent the way they think
   —develop proper attribute hierarchy

   Lack of user-friendliness
   —have explanation capabilities, free-text comments, way for handling uncertainty, text editor, and English-like question–answer capabilities

   Lack of ease of updating the knowledge base
   —have easy-to-use text editor
   —attribute hierarchy should facilitate change

- Test the interface and human factors features. For example, some doctors do not use MYCIN because it takes 30 to 40 minutes to work through a session to arrive at the final decision [11].

With these tips taken into account when validating the expert system, the knowledge engineer's job will be made much easier.

References

1. Buchanan, B. G., Barstow, D., Bechtel, R., Bennett, J., Clancey, W., Kulikowski, C., Mitchell, T., and Waterman, D. A., 1983. "Constructing an Expert System." In *Building Expert Systems*, eds. F. Hayes-Roth, D. A. Waterman, and D. B. Lenat. Reading, MA: Addison-Wesley.

2. Adrion, W. R., Branstad, M. A., and Chernavsky, J. C., 1982. "Validation, Verification, and Testing of Computer Software." *ACM Computing Surveys*, 14, No. 2.

3. Software A&E, 1984. *KES: Knowledge Base Author's Reference Manual*. Arlington, VA: Software Architecture & Engineering, Inc.

4. Shapiro, A. R., 1977. "The Evaluation of Clinical Predictions." *The New England Journal of Medicine*, 296, No. 26.

5. Cohen, J., 1968. "Weighted Kappa: Nominal Scale Agreement with Provision for Scaled Disagreement or Partial Credit." *Psychological Bulletin*, 70, No. 4.

6. Stucki, L. G., 1977. "New Directions in Automated Tools for Improving Software Quality." In *Current Trends in Programming Methodology: Volume 2—Program Validation*, ed. R. T. Yeh. Englewood Cliffs, NJ: Prentice-Hall.

7. Ramamoorthy, C. V., and Ho, S. F., 1977. "Testing Large Software with Automated Software Evaluation Systems." In *Current Trends in Programming Methodology: Volume 2—Program Validation*, ed. R. T. Yeh. Englewood Cliffs, NJ: Prentice-Hall.

8. Gentner, D., 1983. "Structure-Mapping: A Theoretical Framework for Analogy." *Cognitive Science*, 7.

9. Silverman, B. G., 1984. *A Good Analogy and How to Measure It*. Institute for Artificial Intelligence Technical Report. Washington, DC: George Washington University.

10. Liebowitz, J., 1985. *Determining Functional Requirements for NASA Goddard's Command Management System Software Design Using Expert Systems*. D.Sc. dissertation, George Washington University, Washington, DC.

11. Buchanan, B. G., and Shortliffe, E. H., 1984. *Rule-Based Expert Systems: The MYCIN Experiments of the Stanford Heuristic Programming Project*. Reading, MA: Addison-Wesley.

9 Evaluation of Expert Systems*

Evaluation, unlike validation, of expert systems is a topic that has been minimally addressed. Evaluation, whether informal or formal, is an important element in expert system development. Evaluation enables a feedback process to take place, whereby the comments serve as a basis for iterative refinements of the expert system. According to Gaschnig et al. [1], expert systems are evaluated primarily to test for program accuracy and utility:

> Evaluations by domain experts help to determine the *accuracy* of the embedded knowledge and the accuracy of any advice or conclusions that the system provides. Evaluations by users help to determine the *utility* of the system—namely, whether it produces useful results, the extent of its capabilities, its ease of interaction, the intelligibility and credibility of its results, its efficiency and speed, and its reliability.

Evaluation is slightly different from validation. Adrion et al. [2] define validation as the determination of the correctness of the final program or software produced from a development project with respect to the user needs and requirements. Along the same lines as Adrion et al., Yeh [3] defines software validation as analyzing software to determine the extent to which it performs the logical functions intended by its creator. Evaluation, like validation, focuses on the accuracy of the software, but it also concentrates on the "utility," as expressed by Gaschnig, of the software. Validation concerns whether the correct problem was solved [4]; however, evaluation measures the software's accuracy and usefulness.

Evaluations are helpful in determining whether the expert system is meeting its intended original requirements and goals. Davis [5] believes that an evaluation identifies those costs and benefits that deviated from the original estimation of costs and benefits. Even if an expert system is delivered on time, within budget, and correctly and efficiently performs all its specified functions, a user may still be unhappy with it for some of the following reasons, as cited by Boehm et al. [6]:

---

*This chapter first appeared in *Expert Systems*, Vol. 3, No. 2, April 1986. Reprinted with permission from Learned Information, Inc., Medford, New Jersey.

1. The software design may be hard to understand and difficult to modify.

2. The software design may be difficult to use or easy to misuse.

3. The software design may be unnecessarily machine-dependent or hard to integrate with other programs.

Hopefully, a thorough evaluation with the right set of evaluation criteria will flush out these potential problems.

This chapter is organized in the following manner: survey of evaluation approaches, development of criteria for evaluating an expert system, application of the expert system evaluation criteria, evaluation of READ, and conclusions.

Survey of Evaluation Approaches

There have been myriad approaches, through the years, on how to perform evaluation. Some of the early work was performed by Keeney and Raiffa [8] in what they call decision analysis, which consists of four steps: (1) structure the decision problem, (2) assess possible impacts of each alternative, (3) determine preferences (values) of decision makers, and (4) evaluate and compare alternatives. The fourth step pertains to evaluation, and here the basis for evaluation is the expected utility for each alternative. The higher the expected utility is, the more desirable the alternative [8]. Keeney and Raiffa also stress that sensitivity analysis should be conducted during the evaluation stage. Through the years enhancements of Keeney and Raiffa's approach have been developed, such as an approach by Dyer and Sarin [9] called the theory of measurable multiattribute value functions, and another multiattribute utility approach by Ahituv [10].

Silverman [11] points out that two other evaluation approaches are fairly common. The rational man approach is based on the premise that perfect information is available and the optimum solution can be identified by quantitative techniques. The incremental approach assumes that there are no clearly defined goals and no one right solution. With the incremental approach, there must be mutually exclusive and collectively exhaustive decision criteria [11].

Other approaches to information system evaluation also exist. Hamilton and Chervany [12] indicate that there are two major categories of evaluation approaches: summative and formative. Summative methods focus on the outcomes or ends, and such approaches include cost/benefit analysis, use process analysis, utilization, and information economics. Formative approaches focus on the process or means, and include such methods as quality assurance review, compliance audit, budget performance evaluation, post-installation review, service level monitoring, and user attitude survey. Naumann and Palvia [13] have also developed an evaluation technique that combines both quantitative and qualitative evaluation through the Delphi technique.

Saaty [14–16] has contributed to evaluation approaches through his Analytic Hierarchy Process (AHP), which will be further described later in the chapter. This evaluation technique breaks down a problem into its smaller constituent parts and then calls for only simple pairwise comparison judgments to develop priorities in each hierarchy [14]. It allows the evaluator to quantify his/her subjective judgments. The AHP has been successfully applied in numerous situations, anywhere from choosing the best house to buy to determining the best Israeli aircraft design.

These approaches are the more commonly used techniques for evaluating an information system. They seem to stress the need for using both quantitative and qualitative factors for evaluation. Expert system evaluation has centered mainly on the use of blind verification studies and modified Turing tests [1,17]. For example, Yu et al. [18] developed a technique to evaluate clinical judgments as related to MYCIN's level of performance. Abstracts on patients with positive blood cultures were prepared. These abstracts included a summary of the patient's medical history, physical examination, vital sign graphs, medication sheet, laboratory data, and hospital course. The evaluation form (a questionnaire) was "interwoven into the transcript of the computer consultation" [18]. At various stages of the consultation, the expert recorded his/her own conclusions before seeing MYCIN's decisions. This evaluation technique was particularly helpful in assessing the problem of accuracy and in determining future design considerations. Evaluation is an important element in expert systems development as it provides a feedback process for improving the expert system. In the next section, criteria for evaluating an expert system will be developed.

Developing Criteria for Evaluating an Expert System

To perform the evaluation of an expert system, a set of evaluation criteria is needed. A review of the literature reveals different criteria that have been used to evaluate expert system or software quality.

Boehm et al. [6] performed a study on developing characteristics of quality software. They stressed that the characteristics should be mutually exclusive and exhaustive. Toward this goal, they developed the following list of characteristics as related to a software product:

- Device-Independent: software can be executed on computer hardware configurations other than its current one.
- Completeness: all of the software parts are present and each of its parts is fully developed.
- Accuracy: its outputs are sufficiently precise to satisfy their intended use.
- Consistency: it contains uniform notation, terminology, and symbology within itself, and its content is traceable to the requirements.
- Device Efficiency: it fulfills its purpose without waste of resources.
- Accessibility: it facilitates the selective use of its components.
- Communicativeness: it facilitates the specification of inputs and provides outputs whose form and content are easy to assimilate and useful.
- Structuredness: it possesses a definite pattern of organization of its independent parts.
- Self-Descriptiveness: it contains enough information for a reader to determine its objectives, assumptions, constraints, inputs, outputs, components, and status.
- Conciseness: no excessive information is present.
- Legibility: its function and those of its component statements are easily discerned by reading the code.
- Augmentability: it easily accommodates expansions in data storage requirements or component computational functions.

Boehm et al. [6] group these characteristics into seven areas: portability, reliability, efficiency, human-engineering, testability, understandability, and modifiability.

Gaschnig et al. [1] identify five evaluation characteristics for expert systems:

- Quality of the System's Decisions and Advice
- Correctness of the Reasoning Techniques Used
- Quality of the Human/Computer Interaction (both its content and the mechanical issues involved)
- System's Efficiency
- Cost-Effectiveness

The evaluation criteria used for READ were derived from the works of Boehm et al. [6] and Gaschnig et al. [1]. These criteria are tabulated below:

Criteria	Definition with Respect To READ	Boehm's (B) Category and Gaschnig's (G) Category
Ability to update	Is able to reflect changes in spacecraft characteristics and Command Management System (CMS) software functional requirements.	(B) Modifiability
Ease of use	Refers to clear understandability and user-friendliness features, and the software's efficiency in execution time.	(B) Human-Engineering (G) Quality of the Human/Computer Interaction (G) System's Efficiency
Hardware	Refers to the necessary computer equipment for determining CMS requirements	(B) Portability (G) System's Efficiency
Cost-Effectiveness	Refers to the costs and benefits involved in determining CMS requirements.	(G) Cost-Effectiveness
Discourse (Input/Output Content)	Refers to the reasoning approach, help capabilities, and explanation facilities	(B) Understandability (G) Correctness of the Reasoning Techniques Used
Quality of Decisions, Advice, and Performance	Refers to the accuracy and completeness of responses.	(B) Reliability (G) Quality of System's Decisions and Advice
Design Time	Refers to the length of time to develop CMS requirements for a satellite.	(B) Testability

These criteria envelope Gaschnig's set of evaluation criteria, and closely match Boehm's classification of evaluation criteria. The criteria are satisfactory with respect to being mutually exclusive and exhaustive. They cover the important considerations for evaluation purposes—namely, how accurate is the methodology, what resources are needed, how easy is it to use, how sophisticated is it, and can it be easily maintained. They do not appear to overlap with each other.

Applying the Expert System Evaluation Criteria

The aforementioned criteria can be applied to expert system evaluation through the use of the Analytic Hierarchy Process (AHP). The AHP [14–16] breaks down a problem into its smaller constituent parts and then calls for pairwise comparison judgements to develop priorities in each hierarchy. The steps of the AHP are given here[14]:

1.   The problem is defined and you determine what you want to know.

2.   The hierarchy is structured from the top (the objectives from a general viewpoint) through the intermediate levels (criteria on which subsequent levels depend) to the lowest level (which is usually a list of the alternatives).

3.   A set of pairwise comparison matrices is constructed for each of the lower levels—one matrix for each element in the level immediately above.

4.   Having made all the pairwise comparisons and entered the data, the consistency is determined using the eigenvalue.

5.   Steps 3 and 4 are performed for all levels in the hierarchy.

6.   Hierarchical composition is now used to weight the eigenvectors by the weights of the criteria, and the sum is taken over all weighted eigenvector entries corresponding to those in the next lower level of the hierarchy.

7.   The consistency of the entire hierarchy is found by multiplying each consistency index by the priority of the corresponding criterion and adding them together.

Mathematically speaking, priorities are calculated by the process of principal eigenvector extraction and hierarchical weighting [19]. Let us suppose we have a matrix of pairwise comparisons of weights that have n objects $A_1, \ldots, A_n$ whose vector of corresponding weights is $w = (w_1, \ldots, w_n)$. The problem $A_w = $ (maximum eigenvalue) (w) should be solved to obtain an estimate of the weights w. A pairwise comparison reciprocal matrix is used to compare the relative contribution of the elements in each level of the hierarchy to an element in the adjacent upper level. The principal eigenvector of this matrix is then derived and weighted by the priority of the property with respect to which the comparison is made. That weight is determined by comparing the properties among themselves as to their contribution to the criteria of a still higher level. The weighted eigenvectors can next be added componentwise for obtaining an overall weight or priority of contribution of each element to the hierarchy [19]. Bazaraa and Jarvis [20] provide a further explanation, in terms of linear algebra, of the derivation of an eigenvalue.

The AHP satisfies the principles of evaluation developed by Gaschnig et al. [1]. These principles are stated here:

1. Complex objects or processes cannot be evaluated by a single criterion or number.

2. The larger the number of distinct criteria evaluated or measurements taken, the more information will be available on which to base an overall evaluation.

3. People will disagree about the relative significance of various criteria according to their respective interests.

The AHP allows for a multiple number of criteria to be used (principles 1 and 2) and has the facility to quantify a user's relative significance of various criteria (principle 3).

The AHP has been robustly tested and successfully applied in numerous, diverse applications [15, 16]. It provided remarkably accurate results when validated in situations where numerical measures were known [21]. In one experiment four chairs were arranged in a straight line from a light source, and pairwise verbal judgments from subjects were then made about the relative brightness of the chairs. The results, when analyzed, showed a remarkable conformity to the inverse square law of brightness as a function of distance, as can be seen by the following numbers [21]:

Trial 1	Trial 2	Inverse Square Law
.61	.61	.61
.24	.22	.22
.10	.10	.11
.05	.06	.06

Expert Choice

To facilitate the use of the Analytic Hierarchy Process, a microcomputer-based software package, called Expert Choice, has been developed; this simplifies and automates the procedure used in the AHP. Expert Choice [22], which costs $495, runs on the IBM PC, IBM XT, and IBM AT, and is developed by Decision Support Software, Inc. Expert Choice is a decision support system that is capable of supporting decisions with multiple criteria and alternatives. It allows for the decision maker to incorporate his/her subjective as well as objective factors in the decision-making process. It does not have an explanation facility that is similar to expert systems. However, sensitivity analysis can be performed using Expert Choice to handle numerical "what-if" scenarios.

Expert Choice represents a significant contribution to the decision-making process, as it is able to quantify subjective judgments in complex decision-making environments. Expert Choice enables decision makers to structure visually a multifaceted problem in the form of a hierarchy [21]. At the top level (level 0) the goal is defined, such as to determine the satisfaction with the expert system. At the next level the criteria used in evaluating the expert system are listed by the user, such as those criteria cited earlier. The lower level of the hierarchy lists the possible alternatives, such as keep with the status quo (i.e., use the human expert(s) alone) or keep with the expert system.

After constructing this hierarchy, the evaluation process begins, in which Expert Choice will first ask questions to the user to assign priorities (i.e., weights) to the criteria. Expert Choice allows the user to provide his/her judgments in a verbal mode so that no numerical guesses are required (it also does allow the user to answer in a numerical mode). Thus the first question would be: "With respect to the goal of determining satisfaction of the expert system, is criterion one (e.g., design time) as important as criterion two (e.g., quality of the system's advice)?" Again, the user is responsible for determining the criteria and alternatives for his/her decision. If the user's answer to the question is "Yes," then criterion one is compared to criterion three. If the answer is "No," then Expert Choice will ask, "Is design time more important than quality of the system's advice?" Then if the user says "Yes," Expert Choice will show a display to allow the user to answer "moderately more important, strongly more important, very strongly more important, extremely more important, or a degree within the range." Part of a sample stylized dialogue using Expert Choice is shown in Figure 9-1.

Based upon the user's verbal judgments, Expert Choice will calculate the relative importance through a scale, shown in Table 9-1, that is invisible to the user. This procedure is followed to obtain relative priorities of the criteria, in which eigenvalues are calculated based upon pairwise comparisons of one criterion versus another, as previously discussed. Upon obtaining relative weights of the criteria, the alternatives are next weighted with respect to each criterion. For example, Expert Choice would ask the user, "With respect to ability to update, is using the expert system preferable to keeping with the status quo?" Again, the user enters his/her verbal judgments, which are converted to numerical values based upon the eigenvalues of the pairwise comparisons.

After all the pairwise comparisons have been entered, Expert Choice performs a synthesis of adding the global priorities (global priorities indicate the contribution to the overall goal) at each level of the tree hierarchy. The end result of this synthesis will be a ranking of the alternatives—keeping the expert system and keeping with the status quo (i.e., use the human expert(s) alone). An inconsistency index is calculated after each set of pairwise comparisons to show how inconsistent are the user's judgments. An overall inconsistency index is calculated at the end of the synthesis as well. This measure is zero when all judgments are perfectly consistent with one another, and becomes larger when the inconsistency is greater [21]. Saaty [14] suggests that inconsistency is tolerable if it is 0.10 or less.

Figure 9-1

Sample stylized dialogue using Expert Choice

```
          Pairwise Comparisons of Criteria with Respect to the Goal:
          GOAL: USE READ VS. USE HUMAN EXPERT(S) ALONE

                        With respect to
          GOAL OF USE READ VS. USE HUMAN EXPERT(S) ALONE

          QUALITY
                 is STRONG to VERY STRONGLY MORE IMPORTANT THAN
          DISCOURS

               ┌─────────────────────────────────┐
               │ EXTREME───────────────           │
               │ VERY STRONG─────────────    ←     │
               │ STRONG──────────────────          │
               │ MODERATE────────────────          │
               │ EQUAL───────────────────          │
               └─────────────────────────────────┘

     TO SELECT, ↵  TO ENTER COMPARISON.  MOVE BELOW EQUAL OR 'I' TO INVERT
                     - TO MOVE TO PREVIOUS COMPARISON
     * TO CALCULATE/EXIT, <Esc> TO EXIT WITHOUT CALCULATING, N FOR NUMERICAL MODE.
```

Figure 9-1

(continued)

```
                    GOAL: USE READ VS. USE HUMAN EXPERT(S) ALONE

                              With respect to
                GOAL OF USE READ VS. USE HUMAN EXPERT(S) ALONE

            QUALITY
                  is EQUALLY AS IMPORTANT AS
            COST

            +-------------------------------------------+
            |  EXTREME------------------                 |
            |  VERY STRONG-----------------              |
            |  STRONG-------------------                 |
            |  MODERATE-------------------               |
            |  EQUAL----------------------      <--      |
            +-------------------------------------------+

  TO SELECT, ⏎  TO ENTER COMPARISON.  MOVE BELOW EQUAL OR 'I' TO INVERT
                   - TO MOVE TO PREVIOUS COMPARISON
  * TO CALCULATE/EXIT, <Esc> TO EXIT WITHOUT CALCULATING, N FOR NUMERICAL MODE.
                                  .
                                  .
                                  .
```

Pairwise Comparisons of Alternatives with Respect to the Criteria:

```
            GOAL:  USE READ VS. USE HUMAN EXPERT(S) ALONE

                              With respect to
                         QUALITY  < GOAL

          READ
                  is STRONGLY MORE PREFERABLE THAN
          HUMAN

            +-------------------------------------------+
            |  EXTREME------------------                 |
            |  VERY STRONG-----------------              |
            |  STRONG--------------------       <--      |
            |  MODERATE-------------------               |
            |  EQUAL----------------------               |
            +-------------------------------------------+

  TO SELECT, ⏎  TO ENTER COMPARISON.  MOVE BELOW EQUAL OR 'I' TO INVERT
                   - TO MOVE TO PREVIOUS COMPARISON
  * TO CALCULATE/EXIT, <Esc> TO EXIT WITHOUT CALCULATING, N FOR NUMERICAL MODE.
                                  .
                                  .
```

Table 9-1

Scale of Relative Importance

Intensity of Relative Importance	Definition	Explanation
1	Equal importance	Two activities contribute equally to the objective
3	Weak importance of one over another	Experience and judgement slightly favor one activity over another
5	Essential or strong	Experience and judgement strongly favor one activity over another
7	Very strong importance	An activity is strongly favored and its dominance is demonstrated in practice
9	Absolute importance	The evidence favoring one activity over another is of the highest possible order of affirmation
2, 4, 6, 8	Intermediate values between the two adjacent judgements	When compromise is needed
Reciprocals of above nonzero numbers	If activity i has one of the above nonzero numbers assigned to it when compared with activity j, then j has the reciprocal value when compared to i.	

Source: T. L. Saaty, "Priority Setting in Complex Problems," Second World Conference on Mathematics, Las Palmas, Canary Islands, 1982 [14].

The next section will discuss the evaluation results of READ, in which Expert Choice was used as the evaluation tool.

Case Study: Evaluating the READ System

For the users to assess READ's [7, 23, 24, 25] performance, a sample case was run on READ. The users (three) wanted their sample case to be a satellite whose command management system (CMS) software functional requirements have not yet been completely defined. It should be noted, up front, that the sample size (three) of evaluators was extremely small which greatly biases the results. For future efforts more evaluators are needed to assess the accuracy, completeness, and usefulness of READ.

The users wanted to see if READ could help them develop the CMS software functional requirements. COBE, a satellite to be launched in the 1990s, was selected as the sample case. The complete list of requirements for COBE had to be developed, according to NASA's milestones for the COBE project, by the end of 1985. By selecting COBE as the sample case, various advantages resulted. First, the users were able to get hands-on experience in operating READ. This allowed the users to see whether the prototype was easy to use and update. Second, the users were able to tell which READ-derived requirements were omitted from the list and those which should not be on the list in order to see how accurate READ was. Last, the users were able to see which requirements they had accidentally omitted from their list.

For COBE, READ generated 6 first-level CMS functional requirements, 38 second-level requirements, and 109 third-level requirements. Table 9-2 shows pertinent data about these requirements.

Table 9-2

CMS Software Functional Requirements for COBE Using READ

	Number of Prototype-Generated Requirements	Number of Omitted Requirements from the Prototype's List	Number of Requirements That Should Not Have Appeared on the Prototype's List	Number of Requirements That Were Accidentally Omitted from the Users' List
1st Level	6	0	0	0
2nd Level	38	4	2	2
3rd Level	109	Unknown*	10	Unknown*

*Since the functional requirements are still being formulated and there isn't one central document that details the requirements, it was impossible to determine the omitted requirements from both the users' and prototype's list at such a low level as the third level.

The requirements that *should not have appeared* on READ's list were related to those requirements for a pointer mission. Conversely, those requirements *omitted* from READ's list were requirements related to a scanner mission. Evidently, the expert system "thought" that COBE was a pointer mission, instead of a scanner mission, and generated the pointer-related second- and third-level requirements. Careful review of the printout revealed that one of the users accidentally typed "pointer mission" instead of "scanner mission" when READ asked for the value of the nature of the mission. Also, the users forgot to include two requirements in their list of CMS requirements for COBE. These were (1) format network control center (NCC) schedule data and (2) support language interface.

After obtaining hands-on experience in operating READ, the users assessed READ and compared it with the present method of determining CMS software functional requirements, via Expert Choice. Three users evaluated the expert system prototype relative to the status quo. The sample size is very small, but this is partly due to the small number of people who develop CMS requirements.

Tables 9-3, 9-4, and 9-5 show the user results, as generated by Expert Choice. Expert Choice enables decision makers to structure visually a multifaceted problem in the form of a hierarchy [21]. To evaluate READ, the hierarchy is structured as shown at the top of Table 9-3. This hierarchy has three levels. At the top level (level 0) the goal is to evaluate the expert system prototype. At the next level (level 1) the evaluation criteria—response (same as "design time"), quality (of decisions, advice, and performance), discourse (input/output content), hardware, cost, update, and ease of use—are shown and are the same criteria discussed earlier in the chapter. Below level 1 are the alternatives under consideration (level 2). The alternatives used in the evaluation are those previously mentioned, where "KES" refers to the expert system prototype (READ) and "status" refers to the status quo. The hierarchy is shown here to display pictorially the criteria before the criteria are weighted. Local priorities, designated by "L" in the hierarchy, are derived directly from the pairwise comparisons of a group of peer nodes with respect to some parent node. The global priorities, designated by "G" in the hierarchy, indicate the contribution to the overall goal.

In Tables 9-3, 9-4, and 9-5, priorities (or weights) are associated with the criteria. For example, in Table 9-3 quality of the decisions and advice is weighted the highest (.443) for level 1 criteria, per User 1's pairwise judgments. These are relative priorities that are derived by calculating eigenvalues and eigenvalues of matrices representing pairwise comparisons of criteria and alternatives [21]. The user providing the judgments can do so entirely in a verbal mode; no numerical guesses are required. Expert Choice asks the user, for example, "Is quality equally important to hardware?" According to the user's answer, other questions may be asked to determine the relative importance of quality versus hardware. The verbal judgments are then internally converted to a scale of relative importance, as shown in Table 9-1 and already discussed. Then eigenvalues are calculated based upon pairwise comparisons of one criterion versus another, resulting in global priorities.

Table 9-3

User 1 Evaluation Via Expert Choice

Evaluate Expert System Prototype

```
                        GOAL
                        L 1.000
                        G 1.000
```

RESPONSE	QUALITY	DISCOURS	HARDWARE	COST	UPDATE	EASE USE
L 0.143	L 0.143	L 0.143	L 0.143	L 0.143	L 0.143	L 0.143
G 0.143	G 0.143	G 0.143	G 0.143	G 0.143	G 0.143	G 0.143
-KES	-KES	-KES	-KES	-KES	-KES	-KES
L 0.500	L 0.500	L 0.500	L 0.500	L 0.500	L 0.500	L 0.500
G 0.071	G 0.071	G 0.071	G 0.071	G 0.071	G 0.071	G 0.071
-STATUS	-STATUS	-STATUS	-STATUS	-STATUS	-STATUS	-STATUS
L 0.500	L 0.500	L 0.500	L 0.500	L 0.500	L 0.500	L 0.500
G 0.071	G 0.071	G 0.071	G 0.071	G 0.071	G 0.071	G 0.071

Table 9-3

(continued)

EVALUATE EXPERT SYSTEM PROTOTYPE*
TALLY FOR LEAF NODES*

LEVEL 1		LEVEL 2		LEVEL 3	LEVEL 4	LEVEL 5
QUALITY	= 443					
.		KES	= 222			
.		STATUS	= 222			
COST	= 149					
.		KES	= 75			
.		STATUS	= 75			
DISCOURS	= 127					
.		STATUS	= 115			
.		KES	= 13			
EASE USE	= 105					
.		KES	= 94			
.		STATUS	= 10			
RESPONSE	= 74					
.		KES	= 62			
.		STATUS	= 12			
UPDATE	= 53					
.		KES	= 47			
.		STATUS	= 5			
HARDWARE	= 49					
.		STATUS	= 44			
.		KES	= 5			

```
KES      0.517  XXXXXXXXXXXXXXXXXXXXXXXXXXXXXXXXXXXXXXXXXXXXXXXXXXXX

STATUS   0.483  XXXXXXXXXXXXXXXXXXXXXXXXXXXXXXXXXXXXXXXXXXXXXXXXXX

         -----

         1.000
```

*Values are approximate due to rounding.

Pairwise comparisons at level 2 are also performed by the user in comparing each alternative against each criterion. The user needs only to make verbal judgments based upon the questions asked by Expert Choice. Again, Tables 9-3, 9-4, and 9-5 show a breakdown (or synthesis) of the relative global priorities of each alternative for each criterion. The synthesis consists of adding global priorities at each level of the tree [21]. The decimal points have been omitted but are assumed to be placed as if these priorities are in the thousandths. At the bottom of Tables 9-3, 9-4, and 9-5, the results of the synthesis are shown for the problem of evaluating the expert system prototype (READ).

Table 9-4

*User 2 Evaluation Via
Expert Choice*

EVALUATE EXPERT SYSTEM PROTOTYPE*
TALLY FOR LEAF NODES*

LEVEL 1		LEVEL 2		LEVEL 3	LEVEL 4	LEVEL 5
QUALITY	= 368					
.		KES	= 184			
.		STATUS	= 184			
DISCOURS	= 169					
.		KES	= 127			
.		STATUS	= 42			
EASE USE	= 138					
.		KES	= 69			
.		STATUS	= 69			
HARDWARE	= 82					
.		KES	= 61			
.		STATUS	= 20			
COST	= 82					
.		KES	= 68			
.		STATUS	= 14			
UPDATE	= 82					
.		KES	= 68			
.		STATUS	= 14			
RESPONSE	= 79					
. .		KES	= 66			
.		STATUS	= 13			

```
KES      0.644  XXXXXXXXXXXXXXXXXXXXXXXXXXXXXXXXXXXXXXXXXXXXXXXXXXXXXXXX
STATUS   0.356  XXXXXXXXXXXXXXXXXXXXXXXXXXXXXXXXX
                -----
                1.000
```

*Values are approximate due to rounding.

From analyzing the output in the tables, we can see that the users gave the highest weighting to quality of decisions. Two out of three users rated READ equal to the status quo for quality of decisions. The other user rated READ higher than the status quo, as evidenced by the global priority (derived from pairwise comparisons) of 362 for READ versus 40 for the status quo. Discourse, ease of use, and cost were the next heavily weighted criteria, respectively, based on the users' evaluations. Two users rated READ better than the status quo for discourse. The other user rated the status quo higher than READ for discourse. READ, in all three evaluations, was rated better than the status quo for ease of use. Two of the three users preferred READ over the status quo for cost-effectiveness.

Table 9-5

User 3 Evaluation Via Expert Choice

EVALUATE EXPERT SYSTEM PROTOTYPE*
TALLY FOR LEAF NODES*

LEVEL 1			LEVEL 2		LEVEL 3	LEVEL 4	LEVEL 5
QUALITY	=	402					
.			KES	= 362			
.			STATUS	= 40			
UPDATE	=	271					
.			KES	= 237			
.			STATUS	= 34			
EASE USE	=	115					
.			KES	= 100			
.			STATUS	= 14			
COST	=	95					
.			KES	= 79			
.			STATUS	= 16			
DISCOURS	=	72					
.			KES	= 54			
.			STATUS	= 18			
RESPONSE	=	27					
.			KES	= 20			
.			STATUS	= 7			
HARDWARE	=	19					
.			KES	= 14			
.			STATUS	= 5			

```
KES      0.866  XXXXXXXXXXXXXXXXXXXXXXXXXXXXXXXXXXXXXXXXXXXXXXXXXXXXXXXXX
STATUS   0.134  XXXXXXXXXXXXXXXXXXXXXXXXXXXXXXXXXXX
                -----
         1.000
```

*Values are approximate due to rounding.

In further examining the tables, design time (designated as "response") and hardware were the lowest-weighted criteria. In terms of design time, all three users preferred READ over the status quo. This was because it would take only 25 to 30 minutes to develop a good first cut of CMS functional requirements using READ, versus three to four months of once- or twice-a-week meetings, as under the status quo, to determine a sound first cut of CMS functional requirements. For hardware, two of the three users favored READ primarily because it could operate on the IBM PC, which the CMS personnel already have.

At the bottom of the tables, the total ratings appear respectively, for READ and the status quo based upon the pairwise comparisons supplied by each user. The results, per Expert Choice, are shown below:

	Expert System Prototype (READ)	Status Quo
User 1	.517	.483
User 2	.644	.356
User 3	.866	.134

The overall inconsistency indices for each user from the calculations performed on the pairwise judgments are .08, .08, and .06, respectively. An inconsistency index of .10 or less is considered to be tolerable (i.e., the pairwise judgments are 90% consistent or better). It seems that each user preferred READ over the status quo based upon the user's pairwise comparisons of both the criteria and the alternatives.

Conclusions

An approach for evaluating expert systems through using the Analytic Hierarchy Process and Expert Choice was summarized in this chapter. Expert Choice provided an easy-to-use decision-making tool with a sound mathematical basis. Blind verification studies should still be performed when evaluating an expert system, but the Analytic Hierarchy Process/Expert Choice is another technique/tool that might shed some additional insight into the evaluation process. In READ's case the evaluation process indicated that READ could aid the CMS designers in determining a "first cut" of CMS software functional requirements. Its major impact is that it could promote the use of standardized language for CMS requirements development—a practice not presently used in the CMS environment. Standardized language can improve validation and testing of requirements and systems as well as increase the likelihood of software reusability. Again, it must be emphasized that the sample size of three for evaluating READ is extremely small, which greatly biases the results.

References

1. Gaschnig, J., Klahr, P., Pople, H., Shortliffe, E., and Terry, A., 1983. "Evaluation of Expert Systems: Issues and Case Studies." In *Building Expert Systems*, eds. F. Hayes-Roth, D. A. Waterman, and D. B. Lenat. Reading, MA: Addison-Wesley.

2. Adrion, W. R., Branstad, M. A., and Chernavsky, J. C., 1982. "Validation, Verification, and Testing of Computer Software." *ACM Computing Surveys*, 14, No. 2.

3. Yeh, R. T., 1977. *Current Trends in Programming Methodology: Volume 2—Program Validation*. Englewood Cliffs, NJ: Prentice-Hall, Inc.

4. Silverman, B. G., 1984. *Chapter One: Nature of an Expert's Knowledge*. Institute for Artificial Intelligence Technical Report. Washington, DC: George Washington University.

5. Davis, G. B., 1985. *Management Information Systems: Conceptual Foundations, Structure, and Development*. New York: McGraw-Hill.

6. Boehm, B., Brown, J. R., Kaspar, H., Lipow, M., MacLeod, G. J., and Merrit, M. J., 1978. *Characteristics of Software Quality*. Amsterdam: North-Holland.

7. Liebowitz, J., 1985. *Determining Functional Requirements for NASA Goddard's Command Management System Software Design Using Expert Systems.* D.Sc. dissertation, George Washington University, Washington, DC.

8. Keeney, R. L., and Raiffa, H., 1976. *Decisions with Multiple Objectives: Preferences and Value Tradeoffs.* New York: John Wiley & Sons.

9. Dyer, J. S., and Sarin, R. K., 1979. "Measurable Multiattribute Value Functions." *Operations Research*, 27, No. 4.

10. Ahituv, N., 1980. "A Systematic Approach Toward Assessing the Value of an Information System." *MIS Quarterly*, December.

11. Silverman, B. G., 1981. "Project Appraisal Methodology: A Multidimensional R&D Benefit / Cost Assessment Tool." *Management Science*, 27, No. 7.

12. Hamilton, S., and Chervany, N. L., 1981. "Evaluating Information System Effectiveness— Part 1: Comparing Evaluation Approaches." *MIS Quarterly*, September.

13. Naumann, J. D., and Palvia, S., 1982. "A Selection Model for Systems Development Tools." *MIS Quarterly*, March.

14. Saaty, T. L., 1982. "Priority Setting in Complex Problems." *Second World Conference on Mathematics Proceedings.*

15. Saaty, T. L., 1980. *The Analytic Hierarchy Process.* New York: McGraw-Hill.

16. Saaty, T. L., 1982. *Decision Making For Leaders.* Belmont, CA: Wadsworth Publishing.

17. Buchanan, B. G., and Shortliffe E. H., 1984. *Rule-Based Expert Systems: The MYCIN Experiments of the Stanford Heuristic Programming Project.* Reading, MA: Addison-Wesley.

18. Yu, V. L., Buchanan, B. G., Shortliffe, E. H., Wraith, S. M., Davis, R., Scott, A. C., and Cohen, S. N., 1979. "Evaluating the Performance of a Computer-Based Consultant." *Computer Programs in Biomedicine 9.*

19. Wind, Y., and Saaty, T. L., 1980. "Marketing Applications of the Analytic Hierarchy Process." *Management Science*, 26, No. 7.

20. Bazaraa, M. S., and Jarvis, J. J., 1977. *Linear Programming and Network Flows.* New York: John Wiley & Sons.

21. Forman, E. H., 1985. "The Analytic Hierarchy Process as a Decision Support System." Washington, DC: *IEEE Compcom 83 Proceedings.*

22. Decision Support Software, Inc., 1985. *Expert Choice Manual.* McLean, VA.

23. Liebowitz, J., 1986. "Development of an Expert System Prototype for Determining Software Functional Requirements for Command Management Activities at NASA Goddard." *International Journal of Telematics and Informatics*, 3, No. 1.

24. Software A&E, 1984. *Knowledge Engineering System: Knowledge Base Author's Reference Manual.* Arlington, VA: Software Architecture & Engineering, Inc.

25. Liebowitz, J., 1985. "Evaluation of Expert Systems: An Approach and Case Study." In *Proceedings of the IEEE Second Conference on Artificial Intelligence Applications.* Miami, FL: IEEE.

10 Introducing Expert Systems into the Organization and Future Trends

The field of expert systems is just in its infancy. Even though work has been performed in expert systems technology since the 1960s, it really has been only recently that commercial interests have developed in using and pushing the technology. Because of this blossoming interest, companies are jumping on the bandwagon to produce anything related to expert systems. As a result of these efforts, hype has been created and overexpectations on what expert systems can do have been generated. There are many areas where expert systems need to be improved. This chapter will first discuss strategies for introducing expert systems into the organization, and then it will examine the areas for improving expert system technology.

The Value of Expert Systems to an Organization

In the government and industrial environments, several characteristics exist that are common to both sectors. These factors are given here [14]:

- There are too few skilled specialists.
- Increasing job complexity is overwhelming human processing capacity.
- Labor and training costs are rising.
- The information glut is a bottleneck in decision making.
- Institutions need institutional memories to protect against brain drain.

It would be useful to have a way to encapture an individual's forty years of experience before he/she retires or leaves the company. A shift of information processing from people to machines would help solve some of the problem characteristics. Expert systems are one way to encode some of the successes and failures of an individual's experiential learning in order to preserve knowledge and enlarge the corporate memory of the organization.

To introduce expert systems into the organization, several strategies could be used. One approach is for the organization to build an in-house artificial intelligence (AI)/expert systems group. This could be done in several ways. One way is to send key individuals in the organization to short workshop courses and conferences on applied artificial intelligence, buy expert system shells for the microcomputers to allow the individuals to experiment with expert system technology, and even have expert systems consultants come to the organization to teach and train key individuals on expert systems development and the merits of the technology. A corollary to this method is to send key individuals to well-known universities for a formal graduate education in artificial intelligence/expert systems. This is being done by the Internal Revenue Service, where selected agents were sent to universities specializing in artificial intelligence for a two-year masters program. When these agents finish their course work, they will form the nucleus of the Knowledge-Based Systems group at the IRS.

A second approach for introducing expert systems into the organization is to have a strategic affiliation with an AI skill center [14]. An organization might want to ally itself with a university with a well-known artificial intelligence group. For example, Digital Equipment Corporation has very close ties with Carnegie-Mellon University. American Management Systems, Inc., has a close relationship with Teknowledge, a company specializing in artificial intelligence. With these symbiotic relationships, technology transfer can be made, in which the organization can become better adapted to developing, using, and implementing expert systems in the organization.

A third strategy for introducing expert systems technology into an organization is company acquisition. A large company might want to acquire or have the majority interest in an expert systems company. General Motors, for example, has a major interest in Teknowledge.

Each organization must decide which is the best strategy to use. Before the organization makes this choice, it must first decide whether expert systems can play a role in the firm's business activities. It must determine the market demand for AI technology. It must determine the potential external and internal customers for AI applications. It must also study how AI technology can be applied, and how AI can make money or save costs for the organization [14]. After answering these fundamental questions, the organization can then look at its human, capital, and hardware resources to decide how best to harness expert system technology and to decide which strategy is best to use for introducing expert systems into the organization.

Valuable Lessons for the Expert Systems Developer

Numerous lessons have been learned by various developers of expert systems. The major lessons are listed here [14–17]:

- Identify the market and the customer.
- Obtain management support for sustained capability development.
- Acquire experienced technical managers and specialists to harness the technology.
- Secure the participation of the customer's managers and subject-matter experts.
- Choose the right domain and identify real users who will participate in the project; plan for the system to be integrated into the existing method of operations; promote technology awareness throughout the organization, beginning in the early stages of the project.
- If this is a first AI project, pick one that has high impact and small size.
- Make sure that relevant expertise exists and is available, and the expert is interested.
- Prototyping is important—you need a gee whiz system with a lot of bells of whistles if you're going to impress management to get funding.
- Consider using an expert system shell for development purposes—especially for building the expert system prototype.
- Try applying some of the ideas from the systems analysis/software engineering community when developing expert systems.
- Be mindful of the adage: for every shell, there is a perfect task—but for every task, there is not a perfect shell.
- Before investing heavily in AI software and hardware, test out the technology on micros—with the 80386 processor, micros will become much more powerful and useful for some AI applications.
- Plan for expert system verification procedures early on; review by peer experts and formal field trials are both useful.
- Develop an initial version of the system to demonstrate capabilities, with a Go/ No Go decision point for reimplementation and expansion; a fast turnaround time for early evaluation is essential.
- Consider technology transfer in all phases of the project; participative design with a central technology organization will help build synergy and common objectives and facilitate smooth transfer of technology to the users.
- Avoid unrealistic expectations by all concerned; encourage creative applications while maintaining a realistic view of potential payoff.

Not only are there lessons to be learned by the developer, but also managers can learn some valuable lessons when considering the introduction of expert systems technology into the organization.

Valuable Lessons for Management

Managers must be careful to sort out the reality from the hype of expert systems. Expert systems are an important and useful technology, but managers should not have overexpectations of this new technology. Because of impressive sales pitches by expert system vendors and because managers do not fully understand expert system technology, they might believe some of the common fallacies about expert systems. Some of these myths are listed [18]:

- Expert systems do not make mistakes.
- Expert systems can learn from experience.
- Expert systems are deep-reasoning systems.
- Expert systems are easy to build.
- An expert system will replace me.
- Expert systems are hard to use.
- Expert systems can be used for any domain.

These untruths should be realized by the manager at the beginning of the expert system project.

In managing an expert systems project, the manager should make sure that the expert is available, interested, able to stay with the project through several iterations, and able to express facts and her/his thinking process [17]. The knowledge engineer should be skilled in the tools for knowledge representation, be adept in interviewing, and be patient. Rapid prototyping is the usual development process for expert systems building. Through rapid prototyping, iterated prototypes are demonstrated to the expert and users, and an assessment of capability and suitability as a product is permitted [17]. Testing, evaluation, maintainability, and training should also be conducted to ensure the accuracy and use of the expert system.

Managers must be cognizant of the limitations of expert systems technology. Even though expert systems have their advantages, much research is still needed to improve the state-of-the-art in expert systems.

Future Trends and Issues

Expert systems that learn from their experiences, that acquire their knowledge bases directly, that make effective business decisions, that have improved explanation and inferencing capabilities, and that easily interact with each other are on the horizon. These trends are addressed in this section.

Learning

One of the biggest problems with today's expert systems is that most cannot learn from their previous mistakes. Humans learn by various means: by observation, by example, and by analogy. If a child touches a plugged-in hot plate and burns him/herself, then the next time the child sees a hot plate, given the same environmental conditions (i.e., it is plugged in), he/she will know not to touch it. With most expert systems today, besides AM [1], an expert system will follow a given line of reasoning in a particular situation even though that reasoning was used in a similar situation and produced faulty or ludicrous results. Most expert systems cannot automatically learn from their mistakes, such as training a robot not to touch a hot plate a second time.

With today's technology, usually a knowledge engineer has to refine the knowledge base and retest the expert system to compensate for missing gaps of knowledge. Some people, like Lenat [2], feel that expert systems need to have common-sense reasoning built into their knowledge base. With Lenat's EURISKO [2, 3] project, knowledge about the knowledge base itself, allowing the expert system to "know" when a question is beyond its current understanding, is being designed and developed. In this manner a medical diagnosis expert system should be able not only to answer the question, "What is the treatment for body temperature of 100 degrees Fahrenheit, swelling glands, and rapid heartbeat?", but also to answer, "If a hundred-pound box is dropped on a human foot, will there be pain?" [3].

In the Strategic Defense Initiative environment, expert systems will have to reason and *learn* quickly, efficiently, and effectively [4]. Let's assume that an expert system initially determines that an object incoming toward the United States is debris and then, within a few minutes, realizes that it is a real warhead. Then the expert system has to be able to learn quickly and accurately and respond to necessary maneuver and strategy changes. Learning is an important feature in expert systems, and more work is warranted to make this feature possible.

Knowledge Acquisition

Another stumbling block of today's expert systems development is the knowledge acquisition stage. By having a knowledge engineer interview an expert, this knowledge acquisition process has a few problems. First, it usually takes a few months to a year for the knowledge engineer to understand some of the concepts and terminology in a particular problem domain and task. For the knowledge engineer to understand the expert and to ask the right questions during the interviewing process, it is important for the knowledge engineer to have built up a prior reservoir of knowledge on the task. It might be more efficient to eliminate the middleman (i.e., the knowledge engineer) and let the expert speak directly into a computer that will sort his/her knowledge, represent the knowledge, and encode it into a knowledge base. These ideas are being worked on by the Japanese in their Fifth Generation Computer Project [5]. The fifth generation computer is expected to have **natural language** capabilities so the computer can understand, within limits, what an individual is saying. This computer is expected to have built-in knowledge-based systems constructs so the computer can create knowledge bases and expert systems. Instead of referring to millions of instructions per second (MIPS), the computer will process in logical inferences per second (LIPS). This project is quite ambitious, but many resources are being put into this project to make it feasible.

Another problem with today's knowledge acquisition process is that it is time-consuming. In the future, knowledge acquisition aids will be built that will make the knowledge gathering and acquisition process easier. Expert systems to help develop expert systems will be created.

The last major problem with today's knowledge acquisition process is that there is a shortage of adequately trained knowledge engineers. This trend is reversing somewhat as more universities are offering courses in artificial intelligence and knowledge engineering. Also, in-house company courses, as well as short college courses, are being offered to indoctrinate individuals into the knowledge engineering process. With the availability of expert system shells for the microcomputers, more people will be easily able to learn about expert systems technology.

I Business Expert Systems

In the coming years a greater emphasis on developing business expert systems [7, 9, 10, 11, 19] will be created. An expert system can make effective and efficient decisions within specific tasks, and this characteristic is essential within the complex environment of business and management. Expert systems will be designed to interface with database management systems and spreadsheets. Expert systems could be useful as a front end to existing databases or database management systems. In this manner they could act as intelligent interfaces to help query and refine one's search for data and information from the database. Natural language will also play an important role in accessing information from databases. In business, many database management systems have been created and used. It makes sense that expert systems might serve as one vehicle in getting information and explanations from these existing databases.

Spreadsheets, like Lotus 1-2-3, have also been used quite extensively in business. Work is being done to develop expert systems as front ends to electronic spreadsheets, to obtain better explanations, in a verbal mode, of, for example, why gross income went down by 10 percent this year or why expenses rose by 15 percent this month. Guru [6] is a software tool that integrates expert system technology with data processing methods. Guru incorporates full-scale database management, spreadsheet, structured programming language, business graphics, text processing, and other capabilities into a single, unified environment for expert system development [7]. Other software tools will be developed to take advantage of linking expert systems to database management systems.

Expert systems will be used in other areas besides business. Expert systems for telecommunications applications [12] will probably be a supple area for expert systems development. With the increasing role of telecommunications in the home and workplace, there are potential applications for expert systems in telecommunications. For example, expert systems might be developed for the following uses:

- Spectrum management.
- Satellite trouble diagnosis.
- Network management and configuration.
- Equipment maintenance.
- Tracking/navigation of satellites.
- Information management.
- Selection and configuration of local area networks.
- Sensor/signal interpretation.
- Scheduling of tele- and videoconferences.

Expert systems will play increasing roles in the years ahead. Arthur D. Little [8] performed a study and estimated that artificial intelligence products will amount to $250 million in sales in 1985 (.2% of the computer industry), $3–12 billion in 1990 (about 4% of the computer industry), and $50–120 billion in 2000 (about 20% of the computer industry). It is important for companies to start looking now into the technology to stay in the mainstream.

Explanation and Inferencing Capabilities

There is a great need for improving the explanation capabilities of expert systems. Most expert systems can produce WHY and HOW explanations to user queries. However, a hierarchy of, and variety of, explanations need to be developed in expert systems. The kind of explanation that a user may want is perhaps different from the explanation that the knowledge engineer or expert wants. Also, several layers of explanations might be helpful, depending on whether the user is a knowledgeable user or a novice user.

Besides improving the explanation feature in expert systems, other and faster kinds of inferencing techniques will be developed. Expert systems will be expected, in some applications, to make decisions in real time. This is particularly applicable with the Strategic Defense Initiative environment. A factor that might make this possible is the use of parallel processing. This involves developing computers that process data in parallel rather than serially [3]. One goal of the Microelectronics & Computer Technology Corporation (MCC), a consortium of U.S. computer and semiconductor companies in Austin, Texas, is to produce high-speed, parallel processor architectures that use symbolic languages and reduce development and execution time by a factor of 10 or 100 [3]. In future expert systems, explanation and inferencing procedures will be augmented and improved to keep up with the demands of the task environment and users.

Multiple, Cooperating Expert Systems

In the near future, expert systems may have to interact with other expert systems. For example, the output from one expert system may be the input for another expert system. This suggests that an expert system's output must be reliable and accurate because other expert systems will use this output for their input. Testing, validation, and evaluation will therefore play increasingly vital roles in expert systems development. There is a need, in the near future, for structured and perhaps standardized frameworks for testing, validating, and evaluating expert systems. Furthermore, the process of how expert systems can interact and pass information from one system to another is an important issue. This is particularly important when an expert system learns new information or must correct previously deficient results. This new information or mistaken information must be forwarded between the multiple, cooperating expert systems. This suggests that distributed expert systems will play an important role in the years to come. There will be greater needs for developing ways of allowing a hierarchy of several levels with multiple, stand alone nodes of intelligence to be distributed throughout each level. The usual approach being taken is to use a **blackboard** architecture, which is a system architecture that uses multiple accessible processes, called **knowledge sources**, within its database. Other techniques will need to be discovered to handle distributed expert systems.

More Expert System Shells and Decreasing Costs

In the next few years more companies will be developing expert system shells to aid in the expert system building process. As a result of these efforts, expert system shells should decrease in cost because of increased competition. With the potentially growing number of expert system shells and other building aids, the process of developing expert systems will become easier and more widespread. Expert system applications might even move into the home, such as for describing what to eat for various meals to keep within a dietetic regimen.

The coming years will be an interesting period for expert systems development. There is a strong need for increased basic research on issues relating to better explanation and inferencing techniques, knowledge representation schemes, testing and evaluation methods, and learning algorithms. Applied research is needed, too, to test if the ideas derived from the basic research are workable, and to promote the use of expert systems for certain applications. Legal issues on the use, misuse, and nonuse of expert systems might arise in the coming years as more expert systems are built and used [13]. Much work is ahead of us in improving expert systems technology. But with strong motivation and hard efforts, this task will be achievable.

References

1. Davis, R., and Lenat, D. B., 1982. *Knowledge-Based Systems in Artificial Intelligence*. New York: McGraw-Hill.
2. Schrage, M., 1985. "Artificial Intelligence." *The Washington Post*, December 1, pp. F–1, F–6.
3. Fischetti, M. A., 1986. "A Review of Progress at MCC." *Spectrum*, March.
4. Chien, Y. T., and Liebowitz, J., 1986. "Expert Systems in the Strategic Defense Initiative Environment." *Computer*, July.
5. Feigenbaum, E. A., and McCorduck, P., 1983. *The Fifth Generation*. Reading, MA: Addison-Wesley.
6. Micro DataBase Systems, Inc., 1985. *Guru Reference Manual*. Lafayette, IN.
7. Holsapple, C. W., and Whinston, A. B., 1987. *Business Expert Systems*. Homewood, IL: Richard D. Irwin.
8. Arthur D. Little, 1983. *Forecast on Artificial Intelligence Products*. Cambridge, MA.
9. Chorafas, D. N., 1987. *Applying Expert Systems in Business*. New York: McGraw-Hill.
10. Rauch-Hindin, W. B., 1986. *Artificial Intelligence in Business, Science, and Industry—Volume I: Fundamentals*. Englewood Cliffs, NJ: Prentice-Hall.
11. Harmon, P., and King, D., 1985. *Expert Systems: Artificial Intelligence in Business*. New York: John Wiley & Sons.
12. Liebowitz, J., ed., 1988. *Expert System Applications to Telecommunications*. New York: John Wiley & Sons.
13. Zeide, J. S., and Liebowitz, J., 1987. "Using Expert Systems: The Legal Perspective." *IEEE Expert*, 2, No. 1.
14. Thorndyke, P. W., 1985. "Developing and Implementing the Artificial Intelligence Business Plan." In *Proceedings of Artificial Intelligence Conference*, DPMA, Washington, DC, November 21–22.
15. Goyal, S. K., and Worrest, R., 1988. "Expert System Applications to Network Management." In *Expert System Applications to Telecommunications*, ed. Jay Liebowitz. New York: John Wiley & Sons.
16. Davis, T., 1986. Lecture notes on NASA's expert systems development. NASA Kennedy Space Center, FL.
17. Bate, R., 1985. "Managing the Artificial Intelligence Project." In *Proceedings of Artificial Intelligence Conference*, DPMA, Washington, DC, November 21–22.
18. Liebowitz, J., 1987. "Common Fallacies About Expert Systems," *Data Management*, November.
19. Feinstein, J., Liebowitz, J., Look, H., and Silverman, B., eds., 1987. *Proceedings of the First Annual Conference on Expert Systems in Business*. Medford, NJ: Learned Information, Inc.

A KES Inspector Run of the Problem-Oriented Attribute Hierarchy

```
ready for command:  i

-- Checking for Unattached Attributes --
   ** No Unattached Attributes Found **
-- Checking for Direct/Indirect Recursion --
   ** No Direct/Indirect Recursion Found **

Attribute Hierarchy Levels:

LEVEL 0:
   level three functional requirements

LEVEL 1:
   human interface -- level three functional requirements
   ST unique -- level three functional requirements
   move spacecraft -- level three functional requirements
   selecting a target star -- level three functional requirements
   spacecraft constraints -- level three functional requirements
   uses TDRS -- level three functional requirements
   availability of detailed science and mission operations data -- level
      three functional requirements
```

    mission timeline -- level three functional requirements
    user aid -- level three functional requirements
    solar array positioning -- level three functional requirements
    human input -- level three functional requirements
    prespecified group of commands to be executed in set sequence --
      level three functional requirements
    english of command translated into bits -- level three functional
      requirements
    want english and bit configuration -- level three functional
      requirements
    sensor loads to be generated -- level three functional requirements
    real time commanding -- level three functional requirements
    humans want translation of bits back into english -- level three
      functional requirements
    memory image -- level three functional requirements
    input data is part of telemetry stream -- level three functional
      requirements
    need set of limits -- level three functional requirements
    historical record -- level three functional requirements
    sophistication of mission operations staff -- level three functional
      requirements
    immediate feedback -- level three functional requirements
    online operation -- level three functional requirements
    offline operation -- level three functional requirements
    onsite science operations center -- level three functional
      requirements
    historical fashion -- level three functional requirements
    online communication with CMS -- level three functional requirements
    communications on demand -- level three functional requirements
    level two functional requirements -- level three functional
      requirements

LEVEL 2:
    need for wheel speeds -- level two functional requirements
    need for power profile report -- level two functional requirements
    need for constraint checking function -- level two functional
      requirements
    need for data dissemination to different applications -- level two
      functional requirements
    telemetry data -- level two functional requirements
    obc data -- level two functional requirements
    need for installation and verification and maintenance and security
      of data base -- level two functional requirements
    packetization -- level two functional requirements
    interactive mode -- level two functional requirements
    display -- level two functional requirements
    circum -- level two functional requirements

LEVEL 3:
    NCC resources -- circum
    user needs for certain observations -- circum
    pointer mission -- level three functional requirements
    pointer mission -- level two functional requirements
    pointer mission -- circum
    scanner mission -- level three functional requirements
    scanner mission -- level two functional requirements
    scanner mission -- circum

```
user feedback -- level three functional requirements
user feedback -- level two functional requirements
user feedback -- circum
onboard computer coordination work -- circum
user -- level two functional requirements
user -- circum
orbit data -- level two functional requirements
orbit data -- circum
scheduling data -- level two functional requirements
scheduling data -- circum
level one functional requirements -- level two functional
   requirements
level one functional requirements -- circum

LEVEL 4:
   functions -- level one functional requirements
   multinumber of experiments and subsystems  -- level three functional
      requirements
   multinumber of experiments and subsystems -- circum
   multinumber of experiments and subsystems -- level one functional
      requirements
   coupling and interrelationships between experiments -- circum
   coupling and interrelationships between experiments -- level one
      functional requirements
   adaptability of payloads -- level one functional requirements
   real time user response -- level two functional requirements
   real time user response -- circum
   real time user response -- level one functional requirements
   safety considerations  -- level three functional requirements
   safety considerations  -- level two functional requirements
   safety considerations  -- level one functional requirements
   safety considerations  -- level one functional requirements
   concern with capacity of data links and line speeds and volume of
      data -- level one functional requirements
   ease of scheduling -- level one functional requirements
   scheduling frequency update required -- level one functional
      requirements
   ground system architecture -- level one functional requirements
   orbital position -- level one functional requirements
   data interface -- level one functional requirements
   orbital events -- level one functional requirements
   command repertoire and syntax and attributes -- level one functional
      requirements
   basic attitude and maneuver requirements -- level two functional
      requirements
   basic attitude and maneuver requirements -- level one functional
      requirements
   basic attitude and maneuver requirements -- level one functional
      requirements
   control system sensors -- level three functional requirements
   control system sensors -- level one functional requirements
   control system sensors -- level one functional requirements
   user interaction for command requests -- level one functional
      requirements
   command execution conditions -- level one functional requirements
   onboard computer utilization -- level three functional requirements
   onboard computer utilization -- level two functional requirements
```

```
onboard computer utilization -- circum
onboard computer utilization -- level one functional requirements
frequency of user output product interfacing -- level one functional
    requirements
target planning aids -- level one functional requirements
command sequencing planning aids -- level one functional requirements
instrument management aids -- level one functional requirements
initial orbits -- level two functional requirements
initial orbits -- level one functional requirements
initial orbits -- level one functional requirements
spacecraft subsystem contingencies -- level one functional
    requirements
special viewing periods -- level one functional requirements
simulator -- level two functional requirements
simulator -- level one functional requirements
simulator -- level one functional requirements
user independence -- level one functional requirements
data security -- level one functional requirements
joysticking -- circum
joysticking -- level one functional requirements
user assistance and knowledge -- level one functional requirements

LEVEL 5:
characteristics -- functions

LEVEL 6:
nature of mission -- pointer mission
nature of mission -- scanner mission
nature of mission -- pointer mission
nature of mission -- scanner mission
nature of mission -- characteristics
nature of mission -- characteristics

LEVEL 7:
INPUT -- NCC resources
INPUT -- user needs for certain observations
INPUT -- user feedback
INPUT -- need for wheel speeds
INPUT -- need for power profile report
INPUT -- need for constraint checking function
INPUT -- onboard computer coordination work
INPUT -- user
INPUT -- orbit data
INPUT -- need for data dissemination in different applications
INPUT -- telemetry data
INPUT -- scheduling data
INPUT -- obc data
INPUT -- need for installation and verification and maintenance and
    security of data base
INPUT -- packetization
INPUT -- interactive mode
INPUT -- display
INPUT -- human interface
INPUT -- ST unique
INPUT -- move spacecraft
INPUT -- selecting a target star
INPUT -- spacecraft constraints
```

```
INPUT -- uses TDRS
INPUT -- availability of detailed science and mission operations data
INPUT -- mission timeline
INPUT -- user aid
INPUT -- solar array positioning
INPUT -- human input
INPUT -- prespecified group of commands to be executed in set
  sequence
INPUT -- english of command translated into bits
INPUT -- want english and bit configuration
INPUT -- sensor loads to be generated
INPUT -- real time commanding
INPUT -- humans want translation of bits back into english
INPUT -- memory image
INPUT -- input data is part of telemetry stream
INPUT -- need set of limits
INPUT -- historical record
INPUT -- sophistication of mission operations staff
INPUT -- immediate feedback
INPUT -- online operation
INPUT -- offline operation
INPUT -- onsite science operations center
INPUT -- historical fashion
INPUT -- online communications with CMS
INPUT -- communications on demand
INPUT -- nature of mission
INPUT -- multinumber of experiments and subsystems
INPUT -- coupling and interrelationships between experiments
INPUT -- adaptability of payloads
INPUT -- real time user response
INPUT -- safety considerations
INPUT -- concern with capacity of data links and line speeds and
  volume of data
INPUT -- ease of scheduling
INPUT -- scheduling frequency update required
INPUT -- ground system architecture
INPUT -- orbital position
INPUT -- data interface
INPUT -- orbital events
INPUT -- command repertoire and syntax and attributes
INPUT -- basic attitude and maneuver requirements
INPUT -- control system sensors
INPUT -- user interaction for command requests
INPUT -- command execution conditions
INPUT -- onboard computer utilization
INPUT -- frequency of user output product interfacing
INPUT -- target planning aids
INPUT -- command sequencing planning aids
INPUT -- instrument management aids
INPUT -- initial orbits
INPUT -- spacecraft subsystem contingencies
INPUT -- special viewing periods
INPUT -- simulator
INPUT -- user independence
INPUT -- data security
INPUT -- joysticking
INPUT -- user assistance and knowledge
```

B

Sample User Session for Determining CMS Software Functional Requirements for ST (Annotated)

```
% kes.ps
Is a CRT type terminal being used for this session? (y/n) n

(PARSE KNOWLEDGE BASE)
Do you wish a script of this session? (y or n) n

Welcome to kes.ps  Version 1.3 Sat Jun 2 11:42:57 1984

SOFTWARE ARCHITECTURE & ENGINEERING, INC.
Knowledge Engineering System:  Production Rule Subsystem

Enter kes.ps knowledge base:  @add alisa


KNOWLEDGE BASE ACTIVATED-NO ERRORS DETECTED
```

(DISPLAY OF CERTIFICATION OF KNOWLEDGE BASE AND REFERENCES)

certification:

This knowledge base is developed by Jay Liebowitz, a doctoral candidate at George Washington University. It was developed through discussions with the domain experts, Patricia Lightfoot of NASA Goddard and Tom Pfarr of Computer Sciences Corporation over the course of eight months and was finalized in May 1984. This knowledge base has been tested using backcasting of NASA-supported satellites ST, SMM, and DE. These three satellites are typical of future classes of NASA satellites. Special thanks and deep appreciation are extended to Patricia Lightfoot of NASA Goddard for taking so much time out of her busy schedule to aid in the development of the knowledge base. Great thanks are also due to Software A & E, Inc. for the use of KES and the VAX computer.

references:

This knowledge base is built with the aid of the following references:
(1) Lengthy discussions with Patricia Lightfoot of NASA Goddard and Tom Pfarr of Computer Sciences Corporation, October 1983-May 1984.
(2) Rogers, W.C., A CMS Classification Scheme, ORI Corporation, NASA Contract No. NAS5-26183, October 15, 1980.
(3) Computer Sciences Corporation, Space Telescope POCC Applications Software Support Functional Requirements, NASA Contract NAS5-26685, July 1983.
(4) Costa, S.R., Ground Systems Considerations for Projects, NASA Goddard, January 1981.
(5) Computer Sciences Corporation, Solar Maximum Mission CMS Requirements Document, June 30, 1978.
(6) Computer Technology Associates, Inc., Conceptual Design for a Transportable Distributed Command and Control System: Design Concept Document, NASA Contract NAS5-27300, October 7, 1983.
(7) Computer Sciences Corporation, Updates to Dynamics Explorer-A and -B CMS Requirement Definitions, NASA Contract NAS5-24300, June 1980.

```
                    Welcome to
                       the
          Software Functional Requirements Aid
```

(INSTRUCTIONS ON HOW TO USE THE EXPERT SYSTEM PROTOTYPE)

This is an expert system prototype to help determine software functional requirements for command management activities of future NASA satellites.

Kindly answer the multiple choice questions by typing in the number associated with the response. If 'present' appears in your set of multiple answers and is applicable to your response, then always select the response 'present' along with any other applicable responses. For multiple answers, use the symbols '&' for 'and' and '/' for 'or', such as '1&3'.

If you are not sure of an answer, either type 'unknown' or type the number of the appropriate answer and indicate your certainty factor. In the former case of typing 'unknown', this expert system prototype will generate the command management system (CMS) software functional requirements based only upon your 'known' answers. In the latter case of typing the number of the appropriate answer and indicating your certainty factor, this allows you to respond to an answer even if you are not sure of the answer. The certainty factor is your measure of belief in the answer and can be inclusively from -1.0 (absolutely false) to 1.0 (absolutely true). For example, if number 1 was the applicable answer but you were not absolutely positive, you could type '1 (0.5)', where 1 is your answer with a certainty factor of 0.5.

If you want to know the reasons why a particular value(s) was assigned to a characteristic, then type 'justify characteristic' or type 'justify characteristic = value'. For example, if you want to know why a pointer mission takes on a value of 'present', then you would type 'justify pointer mission = present'. After typing the justify command, type 'continue' to continue processing.

If none of the answers apply, type 'none'. To terminate your session, type 'stop'. To use this expert system prototype for another session, type 'next case'. For other commands, type 'help commands'.

Please type 'continue' to begin.

ready for command: continue

nature of mission:

   (1) commandable
   (2) not commandable
   (3) pointer mission
   (4) scanner mission
  = ? (multiple answers permitted) 1&3

If you don't understand what the question means, type 'explain.' If you don't understand what one of the answers of the questions means, type 'explain X', where X refers to the number corresponding to the answer. For example, if the question reads--'safety considerations: (1) complex, (2) average, and (3) simple' and you don't understand what complex means, you would type 'explain 1'. If there are no explanations available, this will be told to you.

multinumber of experiments and subsystems:

   (1) absent
   (2) present
   (3) complex--greater than twelve
   (4) average--greater than eight and less than twelve
   (5) simple--greater than two and less than eight
  = ? (multiple answers permitted) 2&3

coupling and interrelationships between experiments:

   (1) absent
   (2) present
  = ? 2

adaptability of payloads:

    (1) complex
    (2) average
    (3) simple
    = ? explain

Command encountered--deferring current question

Refers to complexity of command loading in adapting to new payloads.

Continuing previous line of questioning

adaptability of payloads:

    (1) complex
    (2) average
    (3) simple
    = ? 1

real time user response:

    (1) absent
    (2) present
    = ? 2

safety considerations:

    (1) absent
    (2) present
    (3) complex
    (4) average
    (5) simple
    = ? (multiple answers permitted) explain

Command encountered--deferring current question

Refers to incorporating, in command management software, ways to handle
such considerations as subsystems going beyond their limits or the
satellite spinning out of control.

Continuing previous line of questioning

safety considerations:

    (1) absent
    (2) present
    (3) complex
    (4) average
    (5) simple
    = ? (multiple answers permitted) 2&3

concern with capacity of data links and line speeds and volume of data:

    (1) complex
    (2) average
    (3) simple
    = ? explain 1

Command encountered--deferring current question

ST is an example of this due to the large number of experimenters'
requirements in relation to the communication aspects of the mission.

Continuing previous line of questioning

concern with capacity of data links and line speeds and volume of data:

    (1) complex
    (2) average
    (3) simple
    = ? 1

ease of scheduling:

(1) complex--few suitable contacts and maximum network facilities
    required
(2) average--several suitable contacts and considerable network
    facilities required
(3) simple--many suitable contacts and minimal network facilities
    required
= ? 1

scheduling frequency update required:

(1) complex--frequent as five to ten times per week
(2) average--infrequent as twice a week
(3) simple--very infrequent as once per week
= ? 1

ground system architecture:

(1) complex
(2) average
(3) simple
= ? explain 1

Command encountered--deferring current question

An example of this is a satellite that has many distributed users.

Continuing previous line of questioning

ground system architecture:

(1) complex
(2) average
(3) simple
= ? 1

orbital position:

(1) complex--need orbital position and velocity required to high
    accuracy continuously
(2) average--just orbital position required
(3) simple--explicit orbital position not required
= ? 1

```
orbital events

(1) complex--many orbital and celestial events required
(2) average--few orbital and celestial events required
(3) simple--very little or no orbital and celestial events required
= ? 1


data interface:

(1) complex--requires very frequent update
(2) average--requires frequent update
(3) simple--requires infrequent update
= ? explain


Command encountered--deferring current question

Relates to the data management system, specifically the updating of the
project data base.

Continuing previous line of questioning

data interface:

(1) complex--requires very frequent update
(2) average--requires frequent update
(3) simple--requires infrequent update
= ? 1


command repertoire and syntax and attributes:

(1) complex
(2) average
(3) simple
= ? 1


basic attitude and maneuver requirements:

(1) complex--continuous three axis pointing by command and extensive
    constraints modeling
(2) average--continuous pointing about a reference attitude with fixed
    attitude references
(3) simple--some pointing about a reference attitude and limited
    constraints checking
= ? 1


control system sensors:

(1) absent
(2) present
(3) complex--extensive choice of simple sensors
(4) average--choice of simple sensors
(5) simple--fixed simple sensors
= ? (multiple answers permitted) 2&3
```

```
user interaction for command requests:

(1) complex--complex set of command memories
(2) average--multiple types of independent command memories
(3) simple--commands from one memory
= ? 1

command execution conditions:

(1) complex
(2) average
(3) simple
= ? 1

onboard computer utilization:

(1) absent
(2) present
= ? 2

frequency of user output product interfacing:

(1) complex--interface support always available
(2) average--interface supported in a fixed schedule
(3) simple--interface supported on a fixed schedule low usage
= ? explain

Command encountered--deferring current question

This refers to how often the experimenters need to interface with CMS
for receiving output from the satellite.

Continuing previous line of questioning

frequency of user output product interfacing:

(1) complex--interface support always available
(2) average--interface supported in a fixed schedule
(3) simple--interface supported on a fixed schedule low usage
= ? 1

target planning aids:

(1) absent
(2) present
= ? 2

command sequencing planning aids:

(1) absent
(2) present
= ? 2
```

```
instrument management aids:

(1) absent
(2) present
= ? 2

initial orbits:

(1) complex
(2) average
(3) simple
= ? explain 1


Command encountered--deferring current question

Refers to very complex and protracted initial stabilization and
attitude control.

Continuing previous line of questioning


initial orbits:

(1) complex
(2) average
(3) simple
= ? explain 3


Command encountered--deferring current question

Refers to very little or no special software or support required for
initial stabilization and control.

Continuing previous line of questioning


initial orbits:

(1) complex
(2) average
(3) simple
= ? 1


spacecraft subsystem contingencies:

(1) complex--very complex recovery planned
(2) average--complex recovery planned
(3) simple--simple recovery procedures
= ? 1


special viewing periods:

(1) complex--major enhancement of normal CMS
(2) average--special software needed
(3) simple--little special software needed
= ? 1
```

```
            simulator:

            (1) absent
            (2) present
            = ? 2

            user independence:

            (1) complex--high independence
            (2) average--medium independence
            (3) simple--low independence
            = ? explain
```

Command encountered--deferring current question

Refers to the flexibility of the experimenter in command and control
activities.

Continuing previous line of questioning

```
            user independence:

            (1) complex--high independence
            (2) average--medium independence
            (3) simple--low independence
            = ? 1

            data security:

            (1) complex--highly proprietary data
            (2) average--medium proprietary data
            (3) simple--low proprietary data
            = ? 1

            joysticking:

            (1) absent
            (2) present
            = ? 2

            user assistance and knowledge:

            (1) complex
            (2) average
            (3) simple
            = ? 1
```

(INPUT ATTRIBUTES OBTAINED THUS FAR ARE LISTED)

These are the major characteristics influencing CMS software functional
requirements determination for a new satellite. Each characteristic
will now be displayed along with its associated value(s) and certainty
factor(s).

multinumber of experiments and subsystems:

```
    present (1.0)
    complex--greater than twelve (1.0)
```

coupling and interrelationships between experiments:

  present (1.0)

adaptability of payloads:

  complex (1.0)

real time user response:

  present (1.0)

safety considerations:

  present (1.0)
  complex (1.0)

concern with capacity of data links and line speeds and volume of data:

  complex (1.0)

ease of scheduling:

  complex--few suitable contacts and maximum network facilities
    required (1.0)

scheduling frequency update required:

  complex--frequent as five to ten times per week (1.0)

ground system architecture:

  complex (1.0)

orbital position:

  complex--need orbital position and velocity required to high accuracy
    continuously (1.0)

orbital events

  complex--many orbital and celestial events required (1.0)

data interface:

  complex--requires very frequent update (1.0)

command repertoire and syntax and attributes:

  complex (1.0)

basic attitude and maneuver requirements:

  complex--continuous three axis pointing by command and extensive
    constraints modeling (1.0)

```
control system sensors:

   present (1.0)
   complex--extensive choice of simple sensors (1.0)

user interaction for command requests:

   complex--complex set of command memories (1.0)

command execution conditions:

   complex (1.0)

onboard computer utilization:

   present (1.0)

frequency of user output product interfacing:

   complex--interface support always available (1.0)

target planning aids:

   present (1.0)

command sequencing planning aids:

   present (1.0)

instrument management aids:

   present (1.0)

initial orbits:

   complex (1.0)

spacecraft subsystem contingencies:

   complex--very complex recovery planned (1.0)

special viewing periods:

   complex--major enhancement of normal CMS (1.0)

simulator:

   present (1.0)

user independence:

   complex--high independence (1.0)

data security:

   complex--highly proprietary data (1.0)
```

joysticking:

  present (1.0)

user assistance and knowledge:

  complex (1.0)

(DISPLAY FIRST LEVEL CMS REQUIREMENTS)
These are the level one CMS software functional requirements, and
respective certainty factors, for the new satellite.

  mission scheduling and planning (1.0)
  command loading (1.0)
  spacecraft subsystem monitoring (1.0)
  data management (1.0)
  operations support (1.0)
  attitude determination and sensor calibration (1.0)

What do you want to do now
  (1) get a justification of the first level requirements reached by
      the requirements aid
  (2) continue to obtain the second and third level requirements
  (3) determine requirements for another satellite
  (4) stop--I am finished
  = ? (multiple answers permitted) 2

(OBTAIN SECOND LEVEL CMS REQUIREMENTS)
user needs for certain observations:

  (1) absent
  (2) present
  = ? explain

Command encountered--deferring current question

Refers to the experimenters having needs to observe various phenomena.

Continuing previous line of questioning

user needs for certain observations

  (1) absent
  (2) present
  = ? 2 (0.9)

NCC resources:

  (1) absent
  (2) present
  = ? 2

user feedback:

  (1) absent
  (2) present
  = ? 2

```
onboard computer coordination work:

   (1) absent
   (2) present
   = ? explain


Command encountered--deferring current question

Refers to software needed to integrate onboard computers.

Continuing previous line of questioning

onboard computer coordination work:

   (1) absent
   (2) present
   = ? 2

user:

(1) human
(2) computer
(3) offsite PIs
= ? (multiple answers permitted) 1&2&3

orbit data:

(1) absent
(2) present
= ? 2

scheduling data:

(1) absent
(2) present
= ? explain


Command encountered--deferring current question

No explanation available.

Continuing previous line of questioning


scheduling data:

(1) absent
(2) present
= ? 2

need for wheel speeds:

(1) absent
(2) present
= ? 2
```

need for power profile report:

(1) absent
(2) present
= ? 2

need for constraint checking function:

(1) absent
(2) present
= ? 2

need for data dissemination to different applications:

(1) absent
(2) present
= ? 2

telemetry data:

(1) absent
(2) present
= ? 2

need for installation and verification and maintenance and security of
data base:

(1) absent
(2) present
= ? 2

packetization:

(1) absent
(2) present
= ? 2

interactive mode:

(1) absent
(2) present
= ? explain

•
Command encountered--deferring current question

Refers to experimenter's need for interactive support.

Continuing previous line of questioning

interactive mode:

(1) absent
(2) present
= ? 2

display:

(1) absent
(2) present
= ? 2

(LISTING OF SECOND LEVEL CMS REQUIREMENTS)

These are the level two CMS software functional requirements, and respective certainty factors, for the new satellite.

```
model reaction wheel speeds (1.0)
predict system power usage (1.0)
monitor system power usage (1.0)
generate composite maneuver parameters (1.0)
translate stored command processor command requests (1.0)
support real time commanding (1.0)
compose load data reports (1.0)
determine fine attitude (1.0)
calibrate attitude sensors (1.0)
monitor special sensor data (1.0)
support special sensor safemode operations (1.0)
develop simulator (1.0)
manage reference star catalog (1.0)
manage orbit data (1.0)
manage telemetry data (1.0)
identify telemetry data by spacecraft time and telemetry time (1.0)
manage project data base (1.0)
build telemetry packages (1.0)
develop facility to maintain obc software (1.0)
support executive display interface (1.0)
support language interface (1.0)
support communications to external areas (1.0)
accept schedule requests (0.9)
generate pointing control parameters (0.9)
verify science and mission operations (0.9)
integrate commands (0.9)
determine real time attitude (0.9)
supply special sensor support data (0.9)
correlate spacecraft clock to universal time (0.9)
perform transponder frequency prediction (0.9)
adjust scheduled times (0.9)
build stored command processor loads (0.8)
provide engineering telemetry data analysis tools (0.8)
maintain flight data base parameters (0.8)
provide reports (0.8)
check maneuver schedule (0.72)
format ncc schedule data (0.72)
support obc software (0.7)
simulate attitude data(0.7)
archive data files(0.5)


What do you want to do now
    (1) get a justification of the second level requirements reached by
        the requirements aid
    (2) continue to obtain the third level requirements
    (3) determine requirements for another satellite
    (4) stop--I am finished
    = ? (multiple answers permitted) 2
```

(OBTAIN THIRD LEVEL CMS REQUIREMENTS)

```
human interface:

  (1) absent
  (2) present
  = ? 2

ST unique:

  (1) absent
  (2) present
  = ? 2

move spacecraft:

  (1) absent
  (2) present
  = ? 2

selecting a target star:

  (1) absent
  (2) present
  = ? 2

spacecraft constraints:

  (1) absent
  (2) present
  = ? 2

uses TDRS:

  (1) absent
  (2) present
  = ? 2

availability of detailed science and mission operations data:

  (1) absent
  (2) present
  = ? 2

mission timeline:

  (1) absent
  (2) present
  = ? 2

user aid:

  (1) absent
  (2) present
  = ? 2
```

```
         solar array positioning:

            (1) absent
            (2) present
            = ? 2


         human input:

            (1) absent
            (2) present
            = ? 2


         prespecified group of commands to be executed in set sequence:

            (1) absent
            (2) present
            = ? 2


         english of command translated into bits:

            (1) absent
            (2) present
            = ? 2


         want english and bit configuration:

            (1) absent
            (2) present
            = ? 2


         sensor loads to be generated:

            (1) absent
            (2) present
            = ? 2


         real time commanding:

            (1) absent
            (2) present
            = ? 2


         humans want translation of bits back into english:

            (1) absent
            (2) present
            = ? 2


         memory image:

            (1) absent
            (2) present
            = ? 2
```

input data is part of telemetry stream:

    (1) absent
    (2) present
    = ? 2

need set of limits:

    (1) absent
    (2) present
    = ? 2

historical record:

    (1) absent
    (2) present
    = ? 2

sophistication of mission operations staff:

    (1) complex
    (2) average
    (3) simple
    = ? 2

immediate feedback:

    (1) absent
    (2) present
    = ? 2

online operation:

    (1) absent
    (2) present
    = ? 2

offline operation:

    (1) absent
    (2) present
    = ? 2

onsite science operations center:

    (1) absent
    (2) present
    = ? 2

online communications with CMS:

    (1) absent
    (2) present
    = ? 2

```
communications on demand:

   (1) absent
   (2) present
   = ? 2
```

(LISTING OF THIRD LEVEL CMS REQUIREMENTS)

These are the level three CMS software functional requirements, and respective certainty factors, for the new satellite.

```
merge schedule requests (1.0)
compile mission schedule parameters (1.0)
process without sms (1.0)
prepare maneuver request data for uplink parameter generation (1.0)
correlate events to power mode (1.0)
calculate solar array power output (1.0)
generate power profile report (1.0)
merge request syntax (1.0)
fabricate spacecraft formatted commands (1.0)
check command constraints and restrictions and validity (1.0)
verify scp loads (1.0)
build mission timeline (1.0)
build scp maps (1.0)
compile error log (1.0)
create operational period catalog (1.0)
convert fine attitude telemetry data (1.0)
acquire initial attitude estimate (1.0)
compute fine attitude and verify sensor attitude (1.0)
prepare data for rmga calibration (1.0)
calibrate css (1.0)
calibrate mss (1.0)
calibrate rgas (1.0)
determine fhst alignments (1.0)
determine fhst magnitude sensitivities (1.0)
calibrate rmgas (1.0)
extract converted sensor monitor data (1.0)
access guide star acquisition performance (1.0)
monitor sensor thermal control subsystem (1.0)
determine initial sensor alignment (1.0)
support opd and actuator control (1.0)
compute spacecraft clock rate corresponding to reference universal
  time (1.0)
relate current vehicle time to universal time (1.0)
control hga position (1.0)
perform actual commanding as related to orbit data (1.0)
store telemetry data (1.0)
manage online telemetry data (1.0)
manage offline telemetry data (1.0)
collect data for transmission (1.0)
create final product astronomy record (1.0)
develop master planned experimenter target list (1.0)
support online communications (1.0)
support communications on demand (1.0)
convert time and engineering units (0.9)
```

compute target and command quaternions (0.9)
calculate maneuver parameters (0.9)
calculate momentum management parameters (0.9)
compute guide star parameters (0.9)
select reference stars (0.9)
merge command requests and directives (0.9)
compose error log (0.9)
separate command streams (0.9)
calculate predicted power state (0.9)
compose uplink schedule report (0.9)
convert real time telemetry data (0.9)
adjust real time data (0.9)
compute real time three axis attitude (0.9)
create snapshots (0.9)
identify observations (0.9)
prepare data for sensor calibration (0.9)
produce data to support sensor calibration (0.9)
extract converted sensor support data (0.9)
calculate sensor thermal model (0.9)
calculate sensor plate scale (0.9)
calculate sensor optical distortion (0.9)
calculate sensor alignments (0.9)
determine sensor star magnitude calibration (0.9)
compute spacecraft clock drift rate (0.9)
provide hga fault isolation support (0.9)
perform command loading as related to orbit data (0.9)
validate subset data request (0.9)
create report of available online data (0.9)
select data for transmission (0.9)
transmit telemetry data (0.9)
create loads (0.820224)
compose mission schedule report (0.81)
perform input editing (0.8)
check celestial and usage constraints (0.8)
generate pointing control directives (0.8)
position hga (0.8)
provide lga selection (0.8)
compute power change (0.8)
expand groups (0.8)
produce command translation report (0.8)
generate attitude reference update parameters (0.8)
select analytical and report options (0.8)
create operational reports (0.8)
compute reference universal time accounting for all delays (0.8)
extract telemetry subset data (0.8)
develop set of constraints applied to viewing targets (0.8)
develop an optimum sub target list (0.8)
manage list of allowable commands and flags of critical commands and
   command mnemonics (0.8)
manage limitations on spacecraft (0.8)
update onboard ephemeris model (0.8)
update onboard geomagnetic field model (0.8)
update programmable telemetry formats (0.8)
update onboard attitude solution and calibration parameters (0.8)
update obc table entries (0.8)
determine solar array positioning (0.72)
create science observations log (0.72)

```
          generate valid header packets (0.72)
          analyze engineering data (0.72)
          check request syntax (0.7)
          create planned real time commands (0.7)
          create software loads (0.7)
          simulate profile (0.7)
          simulate spacecraft motion (0.7)
          simulate telemetry data (0.7)
          query telemetry data (0.7)
          create astronomy output observation set header (0.7)
          constraint check instrument usage (0.648)
          create load format (0.64)
          select desired engineering telemetry (0.64)
          create telemetry subset definition (0.64)
          collect raw and converted subset data (0.64)
          manage conversion algorithms for engineering units (0.64)
          manage list of ground system users and their functions (0.64)
          generate automatic command directives (0.63)
          compose mission activity report (0.63)
          simulate sensor data (0.63)
          simulate engineering dat (0.63)
          do mission planning and scheduling for long term selection of targets
            for viewing (0.6)
          check equipment power mode transition constraints (0.576)
          maintain load continuity (0.576)
          create real time obc table loads (0.56)
          manage software packages and tools (0.56)
          check interdependency constraints and restrictions (0.512)
          provide historical data on orbital or celestial events (0.5)
          manage master target list (0.1)
          manage miscellaneous identifiers of data (0.32)

Do you want to get a justification of the third level requirements
reached by the requirements aid
   (1) yes
   (2) no
 = ? 2
```

(END THE SESSION)

```
Thanks for using this functional requirements aid.  Type 'next case' if
you want to repeat the above with another satellite or type 'stop' if
you want to terminate the session.

ready for command:  stop

KES terminated
A SOFTWARE ARCHITECTURE AND ENGINEERING, INC. Product
```

Case Study of a Business-Oriented Expert System Prototype

This appendix describes the design and development of an expert system prototype for helping an archivist clarify his request and efficiently locate the information he wants at the U.S. National Archives and Records Administration (NARA). The prototype was designed to test the usefulness of expert information retrieval systems at NARA. It was developed to act as an "archivist's assistant" to help the archivist clarify vague requests and then assist in navigating the archivist through the Archives records to obtain the appropriate information per the request. This prototype was developed by DeSalvo, Glamm, and Liebowitz [1, 2, 3] at American Management Systems.

This appendix will describe the steps of the expert system development life cycle, as pertained to the NARA expert system prototype.

Problem Selection

The Archives is in the process of developing a large-scale automated information storage and retrieval system (ISAR) to meet several purposes [2]:

- Help the Federal agencies decide which of their records are of historical significance.

- Index, organize, and catalog the records for future reference.
- Assist researchers in finding the materials that they need.

To facilitate the retrieval of information and better capture the skills and institutional memory of archivists, an expert system prototype was built with the goal of being a front end to the ISAR. This expert system prototype serves the following general goals [2]:

- Concentrate on capturing the way archivists "navigate" the Archives' holdings, because (1) the project team already understands the problem domain well, (2) it appears to be a convenient and boundable problem, and (3) what we learn about the retrieval process should have application to other systems, since the Archives is oriented toward providing service (i.e., retrieval) to researchers.
- Design an expert system to act as an "archivist's assistant" by providing consultation to archivists rather than researchers, to make it easier to limit the size and complexity of the system.
- Use an expert system shell, in this case M.1 from Teknowledge, Inc., Palo Alto, California, to shorten the development time of the system, and save costs (the system runs on an IBM-PC).

To properly scope the domain for this prototype, it was decided that the domain would be a group of documents comprising Department of Interior records for the 19th and early to middle 20th centuries. This limited domain offered the following advantages [2]:

- The records are well structured enough to provide definable "edges" to the knowledge base—places where a query can be easily halted because the needed information is outside the scope of the system.
- The records comprise enough information to provide a meaningful test of the navigation concept.
- The records are frequently used in answering topical queries, so a number of cases exist that show the navigation from one series to another within the group.

After selecting the well-bounded problem for expert system prototype development, the next step involved knowledge acquisition.

Knowledge Acquisition

Before acquiring knowledge from the expert, it was extremely important to understand the concepts, approaches, and terminology in the problem domain being used for expert system prototype development. Key members of the project team for the NARA expert system prototype had the advantage of being involved in a prior project in which the functional information requirements for the Office of the National Archives were developed over two years. This prior knowledge of the Archives' information system was very helpful to understand the terminology, approaches, and concepts used in the National Archives. This allowed the project team to get a good foundation to perform knowledge acquisition for the expert system development.

After meeting with multiple experts, a primary domain expert was selected for the project. The actual software for the expert system prototype was developed during 11 weeks, with 3 persons working on the project. During the first six weeks of the project, the domain expert spent an increasing amount of time working directly with the knowledge engineer. Then, for about the next four weeks, they worked apart except for one or two meetings per week of a half day each. As the system neared its completion during the fourth month of the project, they worked more closely together again, primarily refining the system's dialogue and the order in which it asks questions [1, 2].

The expert system prototype followed the rapid prototyping development concept. This "build a little, test a little" approach required iterative refinements of the knowledge base. Thus a recycling of the expert system development life cycle steps was used throughout the project.

After acquiring the knowledge, the next step was knowledge representation.

Knowledge Representation

Rules were used to represent the knowledge in the expert system prototype. An example of the rules is shown [2]:

```
IF      water rights is-a-topic,
THEN    examine record group 48 first cf 100.
```

During the development of this expert system prototype, the first five weeks were devoted to building "core" software, and the last six weeks were concentrated on refining the user interface and enlarging the knowledge base. The cumulative growth in rules, used either for inferring search strategies or for handling data, during this expert system project was initially slow; then it escalated [1, 2]:

Week	Number of Rules
1	12
2	17
3	25
4	27
5	36
6	47
7	46
8	49
9	102
10	270
11	288

By the end of the building process, the expert system prototype had close to 300 rules in 11 weeks. After the knowledge representation step, knowledge programming followed.

Knowledge Programming

The expert system was implemented on an IBM-PC/AT, with 640KB of main memory, and occupied something less than 400KB of disk space [2]. It consisted of about 300 rules and

1200 lines of C and assembly language source code [2]. The system had four main components [1, 2]:

1. The *knowledge bases*, which are subdivided into four functional modules, each of which operates part of the retrieval process. The knowledge bases are written in the M.1 expert system shell, and contain 4 modules of backward chaining rules:

    a.   Control rules, which control the flow of the program—for example:

```
IF    the introduction has been presented to the user
AND   query abstraction is done
AND   resolution is done
AND   refinement is done
THEN  consultation is over.
```

    b.   Query abstraction, which uses rules and certainty factors to determine the most important topics that are contained in a set of general subjects that the user identifies.

    c.   Resolution, which first matches topics to the general types of documents, such as personnel records, which may have answers to an inquiry, and then identifies specific sets of records in the underlying database.

    d.   Refinement, which allows the user to cycle back through the process if so desired.

2. An *assembly language interface*, which allows the M.1 software to call and execute other programs.

3. *C language programs*, to do most file handling chores.

4. *Flat text files* and *dBase II files*. Text files are used primarily to store the various lists that the system makes use of during processing, including facts and information about the records or the search process. The flat text files contain a list of the research subjects that the system can address. dBase II files are used in much the same way as the flat text files. However, data is extracted from them using C language routines that, under the control of the knowledge base, search and sort files much more efficiently than the M.1 software could. The titles of records series, for example, are contained and indexed into dBase II files.

With the operation of these components, the expert system prototype imitates a simple, mechanistic form of deductive logic with which it narrows down the possible set of records that pertain to the researcher's inquiry [1, 2].

Testing of this prototypefollowed the knowledge programming.

Knowledge Testing

The archivist and the system together identified 100 series as possible places to look for answers to the sample inquiries [2]. Of these 100 series, 66% were found by the system and archivist, 13% were found by the system and not by the archivist, and 21% were found by the archivist and not by the system. The system passed over 21 cases mainly because not all of the series were completely described in the system's database. After updating the database, the system correctly identified 91 to 92% of the series during several post-assessment trials [2].

The expert system was able to retrieve some series that the archivist missed on the first pass [2]. A significant portion (61%) turned out to be correct. The others were wrong for one of three reasons:

1. The series was retrieved based on subject, but was in the wrong geographic area because no specific geographic data was included in the index.

2. The temporary thesaurus created in the system made a weak match between terms—in this case hydro-electric power was matched to the term water-power, which, because of the limited text search capabilities in the prototype, matched on the subject index term "water." Out of 4 series retrieved that way, only one had information on hydro-electric power.

3. A plain lack of indexing—in this case predecessor records to the Bureau of Fisheries were retrieved on the title line reference to fish [2].

Conclusions

Based on this work, it appears that it would be feasible and useful to apply an expert system front-end to the Archives' information retrieval system. A system that works heuristically offers the advantages of:

1. Relatively low cost in terms of system overhead.

2. A way to change the database access schemes (by changing rules) that does not affect the primary information database.

3. The ability to factor in the special insights and experience of highly skilled archivists.

References

1. DeSalvo, D. A., Glamm, A. E., and Liebowitz, J., 1987. "Structured Design of an Expert System Prototype at the National Archives." In *Expert Systems for Business*, ed. B. Silverman. Reading, MA: Addison-Wesley.
2. DeSalvo, D. A., and Liebowitz, J., 1986. "Follow-Up Case History: An Expert Information Retrieval System at the U.S. National Archives." In *Proceedings of the International Expert Systems Conference*. London, England: Learned Information, Inc.
3. DeSalvo, D. A., and Liebowitz, J., 1986. "The Application of an Expert System for Information Retrieval at the National Archives,." *Telematics and Informatics*, 3, No. 1.

Glossary & Index

constraints	facts that restrict the solution to a problem. (p. 64)
control	procedure(s) that affects the order of problem-solving tasks in expert systems. (p. 57)
control knowledge	facts that influence the selection of the control strategy. (p. 57)
control strategy	selecting the next course of action given many problem-solving tasks. (pp. 57, 58)
data driven	refers to forward chaining. (p. 6)
declarative knowledge	knowledge that can't be immediately executed but can be retrieved and stored. (pp. 7, 51)
dependency-directed backtracking	a search method that traces back errors and inconsistencies to the inference rules that created them. (p. 63)
dialog structure	the language interface between the user and the expert system in order to get answers from the expert system and challenge the results. (p. 5)
domain	the application area which an expert system is being developed. (pp. 8, 24)
domain expert	an individual, acknowledged by his/her peers as being an expert, who supplies the main source of knowledge in a problem area to the knowledge engineer. (p. 8)
domain knowledge	the facts and rules of thumb of a problem area of application. (p. 8)
event-driven	same as forward chaining. (p. 6)
exhaustive search	searching technique that tests every alternative one at a time. (p. 59)
expert system	a program that emulates the behavior of a human expert in a specialized domain of knowledge. (pp. 1, 3, 25)
expert system shell	a building kit to aid in the construction of expert systems; also referred to as an expert system application generator. (pp. 9, 33, 83)
explanation	the process of describing how and why an expert system reached a particular conclusion. (pp. 3, 5, 9, 102, 136)
fifth generation	the generation of computers that will be built on knowledge-based systems and natural language concepts, and will be described as processing in logical inferences per second instead of millions of instructions per second. (p. 1)
first-order predicate calculus	logic which uses variables to represent objects only. (p. 48)
forward chaining	a search control strategy that starts from facts to arrive at a conclusion. (pp. 6, 62)
frames	a knowledge representation scheme used for descriptive information and employs slot-and-filler techniques. (pp. 7, 51, 91)
fuzzy logic	uses imprecise or possibilistic knowledge, based on fuzzy set theory, to handle uncertainty in expert systems. (p. 68)
generate and test	state-space search which generates a solution and tests that solution to see if it meets constraints. (pp. 6, 63)
goal-driven	same as backward chaining. (p. 6)

heuristic	a rule of thumb usually developed through professional experience. (pp. 5, 33)
hierarchical planning	a search technique that produces a hierarchy of abstraction spaces, in each of which preconditions at a lower level of abstraction are ignored. (pp. 6, 64)
human factors	addresses all interfaces between man, machine, and the environment in which they are embedded. (p. 95)
inductive learning	the ability to make inductive inference from facts provided by the environment. (p. 133)
inference engine	the program within the expert system that manipulates the knowledge housed in the knowledge base to generate a hypothesis. (pp. 6, 58)
knowledge acquisition	the process of extracting knowledge from the domain expert for developing the knowledge base. This is typically done by interviewing, scenario-building, and questionnaires. (pp. 8, 21, 32, 35, 134)
knowledge base	a set of facts and heuristics specially encoded into the expert system. (pp. 3, 7)
knowledge engineer	the individual who is responsible for the knowledge acquisition, representation, programming, and refinement phases of developing an expert system. (pp. 21, 24, 44, 87)
knowledge engineering	the process of building, testing, and evaluating an expert system. (pp. 21, 24)
knowledge programming	refers to the process of encoding the knowledge into a knowledge base. (pp. 8, 58)
knowledge representation	the method of portraying knowledge acquired from the domain expert and possibly other sources. This is usually done via production rules, frames, scripts, or semantic networks. (pp. 8, 48)
knowledge source	a set of related rules used in a blackboard architecture. (p. 136)
knowledge testing	refinement of the knowledge base, usually accomplished by blind verification studies. (pp. 8, 22, 106, 114)
learning	the cognitive activities involved in acquiring and applying knowledge. (pp. 21, 39, 133)
LISP	a language developed by John McCarthy for symbolic processing. (pp. 5, 68, 92)
list processing	the execution of symbols (strings of characters) and symbol structures (data structures). (p. 25)
logic programming	languages, like PROLOG, based on first-order predicate calculus. (pp. 25, 93)
machine learning	the field devoted to building models of human learning and in understanding how machines might be endowed with the ability to learn. (p. 39)
metaknowledge	knowledge about knowledge. (p. 50)
metarule	a production rule that controls the application of object-level knowledge. (pp. 6, 50)
modus ponens	part of predicate calculus that refers to rules of inference. (p. 48)
monotonic logic	the set of theorems and facts doesn't decrease when new axioms are added to a set of axioms. (p. 48)

multiple worlds creating additional contexts in which to test alternative hypotheses simultaneously. (p. 64)

natural language an application of artificial intelligence in which the focus is programming the computer to understand language and linguistics. (pp. 1, 134)

nodes objects in a linked graph. (p. 52)

object an entity for denoting declarative (and sometimes procedural) knowledge. (pp. 52, 93)

object-oriented language a programming language that manipulates objects used for declarative knowledge. (p. 93)

parsing the process of applying a body of syntactic knowledge and procedure for using the knowledge. (pp. 72, 87)

pattern recognition the process of matching and identifying patterns. (p. 5)

plausible reasoning a form of guessing where, in deciding between two nodes, a search path is followed on an arbitrary basis. (p. 57)

problem space states that can be reached from the initial state by applying the rules in all possible ways. (p. 57)

procedural knowledge knowledge that can be executed. (pp. 7, 49)

production rule an antecedent-consequent rule; SITUATION-ACTION rule; I F-THEN rule. (pp. 7, 49)

production system a problem-solving architecture using a rule-based structure. (pp. 49, 54)

PROLOG a logic programming language introduced by the Europeans and highly favored by Japan. (pp. 5, 68, 92)

propositional calculus refers to predicate calculus involving a set of logical axioms and theorems. (pp. 7, 48)

prototyping developing scaled-down versions of the expert system and iteratively refining each version. (pp. 32, 34)

reasoning by analogy employing analogical inference in solving problems. (pp. 29, 36)

recursive operations that are defined in terms of themselves. (pp. 108, 109)

rule interpreter the part of a production system that executes the rules. (p. 54)

rule-based system an expert system made up of production rules; also called a production system. (pp. 54, 91)

scheduler the program in a blackboard architecture that selects the most likely processing event which will lead to a complete problem solution. (p. 136)

schema same as a frame. (p. 51)

script a special form of a frame which includes scenes of activities. (pp. 7, 51)

search the techniques used in generating hypotheses in the problem space in order to produce the solution. (pp. 57, 63)

second-order predicate calculus	logic which permits variables to represent predicates. (pp. 7, 48)
semantic network	a knowledge representation scheme in which the objects are portrayed as nodes and relationships between them are arcs. (pp. 7, 52)
slot filling	the process of putting values in frames. (pp. 51, 91)
speech recognition	using computers to identify speech patterns. (p. 5)
speech understanding	writing programs that understand the spoken language. (p. 5)
truth maintenance	a system which records justifications for assertions. (p. 64)
well-formed formulas	formulas that use connectives and quantifiers composed of terms and atomic formulas. (p. 48)
working memory	a production system's global database. (pp. 49, 54)

Notes

Notes

Notes

Notes

Notes

Notes

Notes

Notes

Notes